Recipes for Remembrance

A Family Album
Featuring Stars of the
Lawrence Welk Show

Cinda Goold Redman
& Jo Berry

1817

Harper & Row, Publishers, San Francisco

Cambridge, Hagerstown, New York, Philadelphia, Washington
London, Mexico City, São Paulo, Singapore, Sydney

Illustrator: Pat Ronzone
Designer: Allen Eckman White Stone, Inc.

86 87 88 89 90 *MPC* 10 9 8 7 6 5 4 3 2 1

Acknowledgments

I would not have been able to complete this book without the help of so many people. First of all I want to thank Norma Zimmer for giving the luncheon that sparked the idea for this book and for all of her support, advice, and for writing the foreword. My love and gratitude to my husband, Michael, and daughters Jennifer and Melissa, for being so patient during my many absent hours from home. Thanks, too, to my mother, Kay Goold, and her good friend, Betty Wick, for testing the recipes. I must thank Cindy and Glori Popiela for helping me transcribe the interviews and for taking care of my children in my absence. A note of thanks to Margaret Heron for her thoughtful assistance. It is with great appreciation that I acknowledge the many hours of conscientious labor by Jo Berry, Pat Ronzone and Allen and Patty Eckman. Thank-you All. And a great big Thank-You to all of the Musical Family that contributed to this book, for without them there would be no *Recipes for Remembrance*.

Cinda Goold Redman

From the Authors

We had no way of tracing the origin of the recipes submitted to us. We have described sources that were named to us, but make no claims to originality. Every recipe in the book was given to us by the performers and we credit them as the source for these delicious offerings.

Biography of Cinda Goold Redman

Cinda Goold Redman is a concert pianist and has performed with her singer husband, Michael, for fifteen years. They have appeared in many concerts and on many popular television shows in the United States and abroad. A professional chamber music performer, Cinda also plays with the Libre-Temps Trio in civic concerts. She graduated from the University of Southern California with honors and taught piano at the university while she was

working on her masters degree. During her years at USC she performed at a private audience for Princess Irene of Greece, who was in Los Angeles on a state visit. Cinda has taught actors and actresses how to sight read music, and she also teaches piano. Because of Michael's participation in the Welk show, she became acquainted socially with the stars who contributed to this book. The Redmans live in the San Fernando Valley with their two daughters, Jennifer and Melissa.

Biography of Jo Berry

Jo Berry is a lecturer, teacher and free-lance writer and editor. She has authored eleven books and has had numerous manuals and articles published. Her study tapes are distributed internationally and she has appeared on many well-known television and radio shows. She conducts seminars nationwide on a variety of topics such as self-image and time-management, and is listed in the International Who's Who of Women. Jo, a widow, lives in Granada Hills, California with her teenage son, Brian. She has two grown daughters.

Table of Contents

Foreword

When you join the talents of two vivacious, intelligent women like Cinda Redman and Jo Berry, who are tireless in their efforts for perfection, you are bound to achieve great results. I heartily commend RECIPES FOR REMEMBRANCE to you, both for good reading and good eating. I know you will experience the same sense of excitement that I feel as you read and enjoy this delightful collection of personality sketches, character insights, and favorite recipes.

I predict that RECIPES FOR REMEMBRANCE will become a treasure in your home, and will be as much at home on your coffeetable, as a conversation piece, as it will be as a much used friend on your kitchen shelf. It will undoubtedly head many of your gift lists.

Through the years, I've come to know and love each and every member of the "Musical Family." This book will give you an opportunity to become acquainted with them on a more personal level and to sample some of their favorite recipes that we have enjoyed during our "family" get-togethers, and to share them with your family and friends.

Norma Zimmer

Norma Zimmer
"The Champagne Lady"

Introduction

Some of you may be wondering why a concert pianist is writing a cookbook. It all started when Norma Zimmer invited the women from the Lawrence Welk Show and the wives of the performers to a luncheon at her beautiful mobile home park in La Habra, California. It was a delightful affair, which all of us enjoyed immensely. The luncheon itself was delicious. It consisted of chicken salad, an assortment of fresh fruit on skewers, and date nut bread with cream cheese. The decorations were all pink: pink tablecloths, pink slipcovers on the chairs, and centerpieces of pink roses and white spider mums. A single pink, silk rose graced each place setting.

As I was driving home, thinking about the thank-you note I was planning to write the next day, I decided to ask Norma for the recipe for her delicious chicken salad. Then the idea struck me. I realized there must be a lot of people who would love to sample Norma's wonderful meal. That chicken salad prompted this book.

I know you'll enjoy having the recipes of the stars' favorite dishes. To make this more than just a cookbook, we've added Recipes for Remembrance, where each of our contributors share their favorite memories about their careers, families, or their time with the Musical Family.

Dedication

This book is lovingly dedicated to the families and friends of the Redmans, Goolds and Jo Berry—

To Lawrence Welk and the entire Musical Family—

To George Berry (September, 1931–June, 1984), loving husband and father—

And foremost—to the greater glory of God!

May you enjoy

Lawrence Welk

Lawrence Welk

We want to express special thanks to Mr. Welk for contributing to RECIPES FOR REMEMBRANCE. No book about the Musical Family would be complete without him. Rather than list statistics about a man who is truly a legend in his time, we asked Peggy Lennon Cathcart to share her thoughts about the "father" of the Musical Family.

"Mr. Welk is a person of diverse personalities. He is a charming, fascinating

1

man. He has a great sense of humor, is a practical joker, and is particularly fun to be with. He loves sports and is a marvelous sportsman. He's an astute businessman and was very intuitive about his audience. He seemed to know instinctively what they wanted. He knew how to gather the right people around him who had a basic idea for what it meant to be part of the Musical Family."

Recipe

One of Lawrence Welk's many ventures is the Lawrence Welk Country Club Village in Escondido, California. He kindly shared with us his famous Chicken n' Dumplin's recipe that is served there. "Back home in North Dakota, when good friends and neighbors got together for a Sunday night supper, one of our most popular dishes was chicken n' dumplin's. Here's my favorite recipe and I'd like to share it with you!"

LAWRENCE WELK'S CHICKEN N' DUMPLIN'S

Chicken
Clean and split two 4 lb. fryers all the way up the backbone. Remove backbone. Cut through center of breasts, leaving two full halves per chicken. Breast bone may be removed if desired.

Place chicken in pot, cover with water just to top of chicken and bring to boil. Simmer gently until chicken is tender. Remove from pot and set aside. Add chicken backs to broth. Add 1 carrot, 2 stalks celery, and 1 medium onion—all roughly cut—and simmer for about 30 minutes. (If desired, add a little chicken stock base or chicken bouillon cubes for extra flavor.) When done, remove from heat and strain. Save stock.

Roux for stock
Melt 4 ounces of margarine or butter, beat in 1 cup of flour, add to strained stock. Cook gently for about 5 minutes then add 1 ounce sherry wine, the juice of one-half lemon, a pinch of Accent, a touch of yellow food color or egg shade, and salt to taste. While stock is cooking, remove skin from the cooked chicken and bone if desired.

Dumplin's
In mixing bowl place 1½ cups flour, 2 tsp. baking powder, and ¼ tsp. salt. Cut in 3 Tbsp. shortening and mix until mixture looks like cornmeal. Stir in ¾ cup of milk. Put about ½ inch of water in pan with wire rack that stands 2 or 3 inches above the water line. Cover rack with lightly oiled wax paper, oiled side up. When water is boiling, gently drop dumplin's onto waxed paper, leaving room between for expansion. Steam 8 minutes uncovered, then cover and steam about 7 more minutes. Place chicken in casserole and lay dumplin's on top. Cover both with sauce. Sprinkle a few fresh-cooked green peas on top for color.

Sherry & Sheila Aldridge

Sherry and Sheila Aldridge, the beautiful, popular singing sister twosome, joined the Musical Family in 1977 but they have sung together since they were children. Born and raised in the south, they became a professional team that performed in supper clubs in and around Knoxville, Tennessee. The Aldridge family had watched the Lawrence Welk Show for years so decided to research the possibility of trying to get the girls on that program. Sherry and Sheila found out that the group was going to be on tour in Nashville so quickly bought tickets to a performance and asked their boyfriends to drive them, in hopes that they might get backstage to meet Mr. Welk. Sherry recalled, "We had terrible seats. They were way, way up at the top of the balcony."

Sheila remembered, "Our boyfriends said there was no way we'd be able to swing meeting Mr. Welk, sitting practically in outer space, in a packed auditorium with security guards everywhere, but we were determined." Even after the girls were thrown out of the backstage area three times during intermission, they persisted.

They were about ready to give up when Lawrence suddenly appeared through the curtain, looking for a friend in the audience. Sheila grabbed his coat tail and said, "We're a sister singing act and we're real good and I just know you'd like us if you listened to us." To their amazement and delight, he asked them to audition for him after the show.

After they sang, he told them he liked them very much but that he already had plenty of singers on the show. He gave them his business card and told them if they were ever in Hollywood to drop by. Sherry said they took immediate advantage of the offer. "Needless to say, we went out there in about a week. We sang for Mr. Welk again. He still liked us so had us audition for his production staff, who liked us, too, but there still weren't any openings."

They were discouraged, but not willing to give up. They flew home and told their employers that they had a spot on the show so they could keep taking time off to travel to Los Angeles. They flew back and forth three times and always heard the same story. After each trip they'd return home to earn enough money to go back again.

On their third visit, to their surprise they were escorted into Lawrence's office. Sheila recalled, "He told us that his daughter-in-law, Tanya, and the Semonskis, were leaving the show so he finally had a spot for us." The Aldridge Sisters appeared on the first show of the 1977 season and were on for five years. Mr. Welk once said "they deserve the prize of perserverance."

This talented sister team is still very much in demand. Frequently, they do the opening act for Bob Hope. They recently appeared at Caesar's Palace in Atlantic City, New Jersey, and on a telethon in Canada. They are about to embark as entertainers on a Caribbean cruise.

Sherry shared that she and Sheila are working on an album and hope to improve their act and start a recording career. Sheila is doing some character acting and writing for cable television. She recently appeared on the Ted Turner soap opera, "Down to Earth," and won one of the three female leads in an upcoming feature film called "Bed and Breakfast."

Both sisters married in 1980. Sherry married Bob Davis, who played saxophone and flute with the Lawrence Welk Orchestra and Sheila married comedian Roger Behr. The Behr's make their home in the Los Angeles area and Sherry and Bob have settled in Tennessee.

Recipe for Remembrance

Sheila and Sherry both have fond memories of their time with the Musical Family. Sherry reminisced about the first time they met Mr. Welk. "When we met him at the concert in Nashville, we were dressed alike. He thought we were twins. We were wearing white suits. He turned to us and said, 'How cute-a can you be-a?'"

Sheila says she will never forget the time in their lives when they were trying to get a spot on the show. "We could have so easily given up, but our mother always said not to give up on anything, even if the door seems to have slammed shut. The incredible thing is that we had sent Mr. Welk a tape of our supper club act long before we tried to see him in Nashville. You could hear glasses clinking and people talking in the background. It was terrible but it was all we had to send. He returned it with a rejection letter but our mother never told us until we'd been on the show for six months. It just proves you should never give up when you want something."

Recipes

Sheila's and Sherry's recipes were handed down to them by family and friends. Sherry's "Very Good" Cherry Cream Cheese Pie came from their mother, Jacqueline Aldridge, who lives in Knoxville, Tennessee. Sherry says, "She's an excellent cook. She doesn't even use recipes. She just adds a pinch of this and a dash of that. I have to have every ingredient written down exactly. I would love to take credit and say I'm as

good as she, but unfortunately I'm not. Bob keeps saying he wants to send me home for a couple of months for a crash course in cooking."

Sheila says she's a lousy cook and that her favorite thing to make for dinner is reservations at a nice restaurant. The Chili recipe she gave us came from a close friend of the family, Inez Hugg and Slush Cake from her Aunt "Enie" Azolene Vest. The girls had both of these dishes when they were growing up.

INEZ HUGG'S CHILI

1 Tbsp. salad oil
3 large green peppers, chopped
4 onions, chopped
1½ lbs. lean ground beef
1 (28 ounce) can kidney beans
1 (10¾ ounce) can tomato soup
2 tsp. chili powder
salt and pepper to taste

Sauté onions and peppers in salad oil until tender. Brown the beef. Drain. Add soup, beans and seasonings. Cover and simmer 2 to 3 hours.

SHERRY'S "VERY GOOD" CHERRY CREAM CHEESE PIE

9" baked pie shell
1 (8 ounce) package cream cheese
1 (16 ounce) can sweetened, condensed milk
⅓ cup lemon juice
1 tsp. vanilla
1 can prepared cherry pie filling

Let cream cheese stand at room temperature until soft. Beat until fluffy then gradually stir in the condensed (not evaporated) milk, lemon juice, and vanilla. Blend well. Pour into pie shell and chill for 2 to 3 hours, until set. Top with cherry pie filling.

Bob and Sherry

SLUSH CAKE

First Layer
1 cup flour
½ cup (1 cube) margarine
1½ cups chopped walnuts and pecans

Combine the flour, margarine and 1 cup of the nuts and press into bottom of 13"x 11"x 2" baking dish. Bake at 375 degrees for 15 minutes. Cool.

Second Layer
1 (8 ounce) package cream cheese
1 cup sugar
1 (8 ounce) carton non-dairy whipped cream

Cream the cream cheese and sugar until fluffy then fold in 1½ cups whipped topping. Spread evenly over the first layer.

Third Layer
2 (3½ ounce) packages pistachio instant pudding or any flavor of your choosing
2¾ cups milk

Combine pudding and milk and beat on low speed 2–3 minutes. Pour over cream cheese layer. Spread remaining whipped topping over top and sprinkle with the remaining ½ cup of nuts. Chill over night. Will keep for 1 week. Serves approximately 20.

Anacani

Anacani, the energetic, effervescent bombshell whose singing and dancing delighted Lawrence Welk fans for nine years, was born in the Mexican state of Sinaloa. She moved to Escondido, California with her family when she was three and was a budding performer by the time she reached adolescence. During her teens she followed in an older sister's footsteps, performing on variety programs produced by Mexico's Televisa. A few years later, after an informal audition, she joined the Musical Family in 1972.

This pretty lady with the sparkling eyes and bright smile was one of the most popular performers ever to be on the show. Mr. Welk credits her with much of the success of his Lawrence Welk Country Club Village in Escondido, California. She was the first singing hostess and he claims many people came just to see her.

Shortly after the show went into retirement, Anacani turned to acting, appearing in the widely acclaimed film version of "Zoot Suit" and on the "Marisol" mini-series that was part of television's "Romance Theater." She says, "I got so excited that I didn't only learn my own lines but everyone else's as well."

She is currently co-hosting the new, nationally syndicated series of variety specials, "Bravisimo." She and her husband, Rudy Echeverria, who is a lawyer, met in 1978 on a blind date that was arranged by a cousin. Their first child, Priscila Diana, was born March 9, 1984. When we spoke with Anacani she shared her joy and enthusiasm. "Priscila is such a good baby. She's so much fun. Motherhood is just perfect for me!"

Recipe for Remembrance

"Before Mr. Welk first introduced me on his show, he asked if I would mind if he said that I was Mexican. I thought that was rather peculiar. I've always been proud of my Latin background." So for the nine years that she was on the show, Anacani remembers that fans would greet her by saying, "Oh, you're that nice Mexican girl."

Priscila Diana

Recipe

Anacani passed on a bit of her heritage to us through her recipes. If you like Mexican food, you'll certainly want to prepare Anacani's Homemade Flour Tortillas. The Vegetarian Enchiladas are a dieter's delight and so tasty you'll never miss the meat.

ANACANI'S HOMEMADE FLOUR TORTILLAS

3 cups flour
60 grams lard
2 tsp. baking powder
2 tsp. salt
milk

Hand mix the flour, salt, baking powder, and lard. Gradually add milk until the mass is pasty but not sticky. If it is too dry, add more milk. If it is sticky, add a bit more flour. Mold into 2 inch balls then shape into flat, round tortillas with a rolling pin. Drop each tortilla onto a dry, pre-heated skillet over medium low heat. When it rises and has small lumps on the back side, flip and heat for a few seconds until it rises again. Stuff with your favorite filling or serve with butter.

VEGETARIAN ENCHILADAS

20 corn tortillas
½ cup zucchini, chopped
1 cup carrots, chopped
1½ Tbsp. onion, finely chopped
2 cups white potatoes, finely chopped
6 large, canned ortega chiles
1 clove fresh garlic
2 cups Monterey Jack cheese, shredded
2 cups cheddar cheese, shredded
⅔ cup cooking oil

Simmer the chiles, garlic, and onion with ½ cup water for 15 minutes then liquefy in a blender. Stir-fry the zucchini, carrots, and potatoes in 2 Tbsp. hot oil until just crispy. Fry each tortilla in hot oil, but do not make crisp, then dip into the liquefied chile mixture. Remove and fold in half on a serving platter. Top with the vegetables and cheese. Bake in a 350 degree oven for 8 to 10 minutes, until cheese is melted. Serves 6 to 8.

Ava Barber

Ava began singing professionally when she was ten and joined the "Bonnie Lou and Buster Bluegrass Show" when she was fifteen. She went on to sing at barn dances and in small clubs and recorded a song entitled "Atlanta, Georgia," for Dogwood Records. Ava's mother, an avid Lawrence Welk fan, suggested that Ava send him a tape. "I thought that was crazy. I never expected to hear from him. He probably received 100 letters a day. Why would he even listen to my music and write me back? My Mom said I didn't have anything to lose, so I did."

That was in the summer of 1973 and that fall Ava received a letter from Mr. Welk in which he expressed an interest in having her on the show. "He said he was going to be in Nashville for a golf tournament and asked us to meet him there. We went down to the golf course and spotted him. When I saw him, I swallowed real hard, walked over to him, and introduced myself and my Mom. He took me into a tent, sat me down at a piano, and auditioned me there. He kept saying he liked my voice and that he would love to have me on the show but that he usually didn't make decisions without his production staff. He said, 'We're going to be doing a country show and I think you would be perfect on it, so I'm going to have my secretary send you airplane tickets and make hotel reservations.' I kept telling myself that this couldn't be happening, that something had to go wrong. But sure enough, the tickets came and I was hired."

Ava's husband, Roger Sullivan, is also a musician. She told us, "We met in a club where we were both working. He was a drummer in the band and it was love at first sight." They were married in April of 1972 and after the show went into retirement, bought a home in Knoxville. When asked about her future plans, Ava said, "My goal is to sing my heart out. That's what I know best. I can't picture myself doing anything else. I'm doing a lot of fairs and military shows. I enjoy traveling and we just bought a bus. We're fixing it up. I carry my own band with me now so we needed one." Ava also is looking forward to duplicating the success she had with her hit record, "Bucket to the South," and becoming an even better country singer.

Recipe for Remembrance

"I loved the excitement of being with the Musical Family. That opened other doors for me. Singing on the Welk Show opened the door for me to get on the Grand Ole Opry and to make a hit record in 1978."

Recipe

Ava says she likes to cook but that she specializes in "country cookin'", which is fattening and not too healthy. She shared a Manicotti recipe she fixes frequently, when she has time. It was given to her by her

dear friend, Marcia Liebman, of Escondido, California.

MARCIA'S MANICOTTI

1 lb. package manicotti shells
1 lb. ricotta cheese
½ lb. mozzarella cheese
¼ cup grated parmesan cheese
1 egg
2 tsp. sugar
1 Tbsp. chopped parsley
1 lb. lean ground beef
1 (32 ounce) jar Italian sauce

Cook the manicotti according to package directions. Mix the cheeses, sugar and parsley then stuff into the shells. Arrange in a baking dish and set aside. Brown and drain the ground beef then stir in the Italian sauce and pour over the shells. Cover with foil and bake at 400 degrees for 45–50 minutes. Remove foil the last 10 minutes to brown. Serves 6 to 8.

Barbara Boylan

Barbara Boylan is fondly remembered by fans everywhere as Bobby Burgess' first dancing partner. They performed together on the Lawrence Welk Show from 1960 to 1967 but had been trained in their craft and were dancing together long before that. "Bobby and I were like brother and sister," Barbara recalled. "We had grown up together. I spent every holiday at his house or the other way around. And we were just the best of pals."

14

Barbara met her husband Greg, who is now a human resource director for a major corporation, when he appeared on the show in the mid-sixties as a singer with "The Blenders." "Of course, everybody thought Bobby and I were to be married so it came as a very big shock when I married Greg."

A devoted wife, homemaker and mother to their son, David, and daughter, Diane (who is named after Dee Dee Lennon), Barbara says she will never stop being a dancer. She teaches dance and has seventy-five students, ranging from little children through adult.

Recipe for Remembrance

"Bobby and I started dancing together when we were twelve. We would go to the Steel Pier, which later became the Hollywood Palladium. That's where Lawrence saw us in the audience. He was amazed that, as young as we were, we were doing ballroom dancing. He sponsored a "Calcutta" contest and Bobby and I won. Our reward was to be on the show. He was so pleased that he let us come back. We did the twist to another one of his hits, "Yellowbird," so he invited us back the following week. Every week for six months we came up with a new routine and he kept asking us back. We created our own dances because the show didn't have a choreographer. We sort of created a job for ourselves. We were right out of high school when we became regulars. Lawrence called us his dancing teenagers. It was hard work but great fun!"

Recipes

Before marrying Greg, Barbara never cooked. "Once we were married I was busy trying to learn how to boil eggs," she confessed. "I was terribly proud of the first time I made a tuna casserole, until Greg took a bite and said, 'Gee, what's this?' When I rather indignantly told him it was a tuna casserole, he asked, 'Where's the tuna?'"

Greg and Barbara (Boylan) Dixon

Barbara's cooking skills have greatly improved since then. Her Chocolate Bundt Cake is one her husband and children ask for frequently. It's simple to make and tastes great. The Mud Pie is David's and Dee Dee's birthday favorite. We suggest that when you sample these delicacies, you throw caution to the wind and forget about counting calories!

CHOCOLATE SOUR CREAM BUNDT CAKE

1 package chocolate fudge cake mix
1 (3½ ounce) package chocolate or vanilla instant pudding
½ cup sour cream
½ cup salad oil
½ cup warm water
4 eggs
1 Tbsp. instant coffee (optional)
1½ cups semi-sweet chocolate chips

Place all ingredients except chocolate chips in a large mixing bowl and beat at medium speed for 5 minutes. Add the chocolate chips and mix well with a spoon. Bake in a well-greased, floured bundt pan for 50 minutes at 350 degrees. Cool in pan then place on a cake plate and sprinkle with powdered sugar.

MUD PIE

Crust
18 Oreo cookies, finely crushed
¼ cup melted butter
½ gallon chocolate OR chocolate mint ice cream, softened

Mix cookies and butter. Put into a spring form pan and freeze. When crust is firmly frozen, add ½ gallon softened chocolate or chocolate mint ice cream and freeze until solid.

Topping
4 (1 ounce) squares semi-sweet chocolate
½ cup butter
2 cups sifted, confectioners sugar
½ cup evaporated milk

Melt chocolate and butter in a double boiler. Stir in confectioners sugar then slowly blend in the evaporated milk. Heat until ingredients are well blended. Cool. Spread half of the sauce over the frozen ice cream layer and freeze until firm. To serve, top individual pieces with remaining chocolate sauce, whipped cream and a maraschino cherry.

Bobby Burgess

obby Burgess was the featured dancing star of the Lawrence
Welk television program for twenty-one years. Bobby's dancing
career began, when as a pre-schooler, he started taking dancing lessons.
By the time he was thirteen he had appeared in over seventy-five tele-
vision shows and had been a member of Walt Disney's original troupe of
Mouseketeers for four years. Bobby reminisced, "I had been dancing since I

was four. I did seventy-five amateur television shows before I became a professional dancer. Some agent saw me on one of the shows in Los Angeles and called the station to book me. The first job I went out for was a toothpaste commercial with Ozzie and Harriet. A couple of years later I got the Mouseketeers. There was a time when I went to college, joined a fraternity, and lived a somewhat normal life, but I was always going on interviews and doing television."

While at Disney, Bobby attended the studio school through the eleventh grade. In his senior year of high school, he returned to Polytechnic High School in Long Beach and graduated in 1959. That fall he entered Long Beach State College, but the stress of his work forced him to drop out when he was nine credits short of a degree in Theater Arts.

At a dancing school in his hometown of Long Beach, California, fate intervened and handed him a ready-made partner, Barbara Boylan. Their teacher paired her and Bobby for instruction in ballroom dancing. Ideal partners from the outset, they vied against countless other ballroom couples in competitions all across the country. They scored a grand coup by being named king and queen of the National Grand Medal Ball, winning over some five-thousand other couples.

When Barbara left the Welk Show in 1967 to get married, Bobby searched and found pretty Cissy King of Albuquerque, New Mexico, who became his new dancing partner, and together they continued the tradition as dancing stars of Lawrence Welk's popular television program.

Meanwhile, Bobby met Kristie Floren, daughter of Lawrence's accordionist, Myron Floren. Bobby told us about their wedding. "We were married on Valentine's Day in 1971 and had 1200 people at our wedding, 650 people for a sit down dinner and dance in a red and pink ballroom. Some fan magazine decided to do an exclusive about it and asked if they could put guards outside the church. We were surprised but told them to go ahead. We found out it was a great idea because so many fans showed up."

When Cissy left the fold in December of 1978, Bobby began another search to find a suitable partner. That's when he discovered Elaine Niverson in Houston, Texas. They still perform together.

Bobby is always actively pursuing his career. "I'm still dancing concert tours. Right now I'm taking a musical comedy workshop, which I'm really enjoying. I'm doing ballads and things I've always wanted to do: some acting, some singing, which is really fun. I'd love to do some kind of a musical comedy. When I'm not traveling in my work, my main hobby is to travel with Kristie. Our favorite place has been Bali in Indonesia because the dancing was so unique and the culture so primitive."

Above all, Bobby is a family man. "Of course, number one to me is the family and my kids. Now that I've had some time off, I've really enjoyed getting in touch with my children; taking them to school and that kind of thing. Now they think of me as the dad who gets up to make breakfast. It's fun." Between trips, Bobby and Kristie make their home in the Los Angeles area with their three children, Becki, Robert and Wendi.

Recipe for Remembrance

Bobby has many warm memories about his time with the Musical Family. Some incidents that seemed catastrophic at the moment are extremely humorous in retrospect. "I remember a time in Waterloo, Iowa when I was doing a tap routine and I did the splits and ripped my pants in back. It was at the end of the number and luckily I was dancing in a big arena so the audience was not too close, but I finished the dance holding my pants."

Kristie and Bobby recalled a time when their lives touched in a unique way long before romance entered the picture. Bobby says it must have been fate! Kristie shared her recollection of the incident. "My dad used to do concerts at the Marine Auditorium in Inglewood to raise money for our church. I think I was in elementary school at the time and our class must have been singing because we were sitting in the front row in a group.

Maybe we were in a choir or something. Anyway, Bob was dancing with Barbara and her shoe flew off and hit me. I never told very many people because I was so embarrassed, I turned beet red. But that was the first time Bobby and I connected."

Recipe

The cooks in our test kitchen wrote "Yum! Delicious!" at the top of this Baked Stuffed Shrimp recipe. It's one Kristie picked up when she and Bobby were in New England. "I had to have it everyday. A friend who lives back there sent me the recipe, which I changed a bit. It's one of our favorites." We're sure it will be one of yours, too.

BAKED STUFFED SHRIMP

16 fresh jumbo shrimp
½–¾ cup shredded, fresh crab meat
2 cups Ritz cracker crumbs
½ cup (1 cube) butter
3 Tbsp. parmesan cheese
1 Tbsp. fresh lemon juice
½ tsp. garlic salt

Shell the shrimp, leaving only the tails. Make a small slit in the center of each and stuff with crab meat. Line the shrimp, tails up, in an oven-to-table baking dish. In a saucepan, melt ½ cup butter. Add the cracker crumbs and stir until moist and crumbly. Add the parmesan cheese, lemon juice, and garlic salt. Sprinkle all of the crumb mixture over the shrimp. Cover with aluminum foil and bake at 350 degrees for 20 minutes. Remove foil and broil until the shrimp is golden brown. Serve with dip. Serves 4.

Dip

½ cup (1 cube) butter
1 T. parmesan cheese
⅛ tsp. garlic powder
4 fresh lemon wedges

Divide one cube of butter equally among four individual serving ramekin dishes. Add the cheese and garlic powder in equal amounts in each dish then set in the oven until the butter melts. Stir well. Serve with fresh lemon wedges.

Bobby with Becki and Robert holding baby Wendi

l. to r. Kristie, Wendi, Bobby, Robert and Becki

Jo Ann Castle

Fans remember Jo Ann Castle as the bouncy blonde piano-playing dynamo with the infectious personality and contagious smile who "tickled the ivories" for a decade on the Lawrence Welk Show. Born in Bakersfield, California, Jo Ann started tap dancing when she was three. By the time she was five, she was taking piano lessons and has been performing since she was ten years old. She left the Musical Family in November of 1969 to rest and raise her family.

She met her present husband, Bill Holloway, in March of 1978 when she was performing in a club in Hot Springs, Arkansas. "He took me to dinner and we fell in love, really just about the first or second day after we'd met. We were with each other the whole week in Hot Springs then I came back to California. We talked on the phone constantly for two weeks then he came out here and we were married six months later."

After a brief hiatus in the mid-seventies, Jo Ann again zealously tackled her career. Recently she's returned to country music. She's thrilled with this new approach. "I'm writing my own songs and I've done my first album. I'm doing a lot of concerts and conventions and some fairs. I have my own band and I'm doing television commercials."

As for her goal for the future, she says it is "to entertain for the rest of my life!" Jo Ann and Bill make their home in Hot Springs, Arkansas with her children, Joanie and Billy Roeschlein, who both play the piano and practice an hour every morning before leaving for school.

Recipe for Remembrance

l. to r. Billy, Jo Ann, Bill and Joanie

Life hasn't been all sunshine and roses for Jo Ann. She has battled a weight problem all of her life and was gracious enough to share that struggle, and her triumph over it, with us.

"I weighed 300 pounds when I met my husband. He gave me strength, and so did my daughter who died. (Jo Ann's daughter, who passed away in 1978, was mentally retarded and had cerebral palsy) I lost 150 pounds. I took my time, about a year and a half. I stayed the same for a while then recently lost the final 15 pounds. I had that old body for so long! I don't want it back. I get on a scale every single day."

When asked how she did it, Jo Ann said, "In order to permanently lose weight, first you have to like yourself. After you take care of that, everything kind of falls into place. As for eating, you have to change your approach to food. There is no way that you have to give up anything. Just eat half portions. I'm concerned about how everybody goes on fad diets. I went on all of those but nobody will eat that way for the rest of her life. I even tried the hard-boiled egg and grapefruit diet and sat there dying while everyone else was eating spaghetti."

"All I did to take off my weight permanently was to use a smaller plate, take half-sized portions, and eat slowly. It takes twenty minutes for the appetite signal to reach your brain and tell it you're full. If you eat slowly, you give your body a chance to work in your favor."

Recipes

Jo Ann's recipes are custom-fitted to her busy lifestyle. She calls them self-explanatory quickies. We call them delicous!

JALAPEÑO CORNBREAD

1 cup cornmeal
½ tsp. baking soda
¾ tsp. salt
1 (16 ounce) can cream-style corn
2 eggs, beaten
¼ cup bacon drippings
1 cup milk
½ lb. shredded cheddar cheese
1 onion, chopped
1 (6 ounce) can diced Ortega chiles
2 jalapeño chiles, chopped.

Stir cornmeal, soda, and salt together in mixing bowl. Add the corn, eggs, drippings and milk. Stir until well mixed and dry ingredients are moistened. Pour half the batter into a greased, 9" square baking pan. Combine the cheese, onion and chiles, and sprinkle evenly over the batter. Top with remaining batter.

Bake at 350 degrees for 45 minutes or until a toothpick inserted in the center comes out clean. Serve hot. Serves 9.

SOUTHERN STYLE SLOW COOKER BARBEQUED SPARERIBS

4 lbs. lean spareribs, cut into riblets
1 cup water
1 tsp. salt
1 cup catsup

Jo Ann Castle

½ cup dark corn syrup
½ cup cider vinegar
¼ cup onion, chopped
2 tsp. seasoned salt

Put ribs, water and salt in a 4 quart crock-pot. Cover and cook on low for 8 to 10 hours. About one hour before serving, make the sauce. Combine the catsup, corn syrup, vinegar, onion and seasoned salt in a small saucepan and simmer for 15 minutes. Remove the ribs from the crockpot and drain well on paper towel. Place ribs on the rack of a broiler pan and brush with the glaze. Broil 6 inches below heat until ribs are brown (about 15 minutes) turning and basting once. They can also be broiled on an outdoor grill. Makes 4 to 6 servings.

JO ANN CASTLE'S BEEF TOSTADAS

1 lb. lean ground beef
1 medium onion, chopped
1 clove garlic, minced
1 (4 ounce) can diced, green Ortega chiles
1 tsp. salt
¼ tsp. pepper
½ tsp. crumbled leaf oregano
2 Tbsp. flour
1 cup beef broth
6 corn tortillas
1 cup shredded Monterey Jack cheese
2 cups shredded iceberg lettuce
1 cup guacamole
1 cup sour cream

Cook beef, onion and garlic until brown. Drain off fat and add the chiles, salt, pepper and oregano. In a separate container, combine the flour and beef broth, stirring until completely smooth. Add to the meat mixture and cook over medium heat until thickened (approximately five minutes). Fry the tortillas in hot oil until crisp. Top with meat, cheese and lettuce, then garnish with guacamole and sour cream.

Miriam and George

George Cates

George Cates was born and schooled in the Bronx in New York. He attended New York University and served in the Navy for four years as an instructor at the Navy School of Music in Washington D.C. He also directed the band at the Wave Training Station at Hunter College, New York. He later played and arranged for many name bands, including Russ Morgan, Harry Busse, and Dick Stabile, as well as fronting bands of his own from time to time.

During the ten years he was west coast head of Coral Records, he did arrangements for Teresa Brewer, the McGuire Sisters, the Andrews Sisters, Bing Crosby, and Danny Kaye. He joined the Welk organization as Music Director in 1951, handling all music for recordings and television shows. In recent years George started directing the band "on camera." His high-voltage personality and tremendous sense of humor gave him firm control of one of the finest orchestras in the country.

George has two grown children, a daughter, Gail, and a son, Richard. Widowed several years ago, he is now a comparative newlywed, enjoying life with his lovely second wife, Miriam. Her graciousness and warmth blended perfectly with the friendly personalities of the Musical Family.

Recipes

We know you'll enjoy the mouthwatering, tantalizingly different recipe for George Cate's Favorite Chicken. And you can't beat his Ice Cream Bombé for simplicity and taste.

GEORGE CATE'S FAVORITE CHICKEN

2 frying chickens, cut up, or 12 chicken breasts
1 envelope dry onion soup mix
1 (8 ounce) bottle French salad dressing
1 (16 ounce) can whole berry cranberry sauce

Combine the soup mix, salad dressing and cranberry sauce. Add the chicken. Cover and marinate in the refrigerator for 6 to 8 hours. To cook, pour half of the marinade into a large baking dish. Reserve the rest. Add the chicken and bake in a 350 degree oven for 1½ hours, uncovered, basting often with the remaining marinade. Serve over rice. Serves 8–12, depending on appetites.

ICE CREAM BOMBÉ

2 quarts raspberry sherbet
3 quarts vanilla ice cream
1 cup seedless white raisins
1 cup brandy

Marinate the raisins for 8 hours in the brandy. Soften the sherbet and spread into a chilled mold. Freeze until firm. Drain the raisins and stir into softened vanilla ice cream then spread onto frozen sherbet. Cover and freeze 6 to 8 hours until hardened. Unmold just before serving.

Dick Dale

Dick Dale, known to his peers as "Mr. Personality," was with the Lawrence Welk Orchestra almost from its inception. He joined when Lawrence was on tour in Clinton, Iowa in 1951. Born and raised in Iowa, he served in the Navy during World War II then toured with small "territory bands" in the midwest, playing for local dances. Lawrence heard him perform in Newhall, Minnesota and asked him to join his group. Dick was a jack-of-all-trades and says he did everything from playing saxophone and singing to loading instruments on the truck. He also played Santa to the children on the yearly Christmas shows.

Dick married his wife Marguerite in 1949. They moved to Los Angeles in August of 1951 and still make their home in Southern California. They have three sons, a daughter, and two grandchildren.

After thirty-two years with the show, Dick still is not ready to retire. He is doing concert tours with other members of the Musical Family and somtimes mobilizes a small combo of his own to play for dances or conventions.

Recipe for Remembrance

Dick reminisced that when he joined the band in 1951, "It was small, with a lot of nice guys who were good musicians. We had five saxes, four brass instruments, a girl singer, two male vocalists, and a whistler. We had a lot of fun together. It was a very close group. We started out doing a local television show at KTLA in Los Angeles for Laura Scudder's potato chips, then the Southern California Dodge dealers sponsored us and eventually the show went national."

Before baking mix in:
2 beaten eggs
1 tsp. salt
1 tsp. almond extract (optional)

Drop by teaspoonful, 2 inches apart, onto a greased baking sheet. Bake at 325 degrees for 15 minutes. Store tightly covered.

Recipes

Dick appreciates Marguerite's good cooking and would rather eat food than prepare it. Bernice Stone's Oatmeal Cookies, a snackin' favorite with a distinct, chewy texture, are from a former neighbor whose children went to school with his. The Beef Ribs, a mainstay at the Dale household, are mouth-watering delicious and company good!

BERNICE STONE'S OATMEAL COOKIES

In a large bowl, mix together:
4 cups quick-cooking oats
2 cups firmly packed brown sugar
1 cup salad oil

Let stand in the refrigerator for 12 hours or overnight

BEEF RIBS
1 cup cider vinegar
½ cup honey
2 Tbsp. Worcestershire sauce
½ cup catsup
1 tsp. salt
1 tsp dry mustard
1 tsp. paprika
¼ tsp. black pepper
1 clove minced garlic
4 lbs. beef ribs

Combine all ingredients except the ribs in a saucepan. Bring to a boil then reduce heat and cover and simmer for 15 minutes. Arrange the ribs in a single layer baking pan. Pour the hot marinade over the meat. Cover and let stand for 1 hour. Drain, reserving the excess marinade. Bake the ribs at 325 degrees for 1 hour. While cooking, turn the ribs frequently and baste often with the marinade. Serves 4–6.

Bob Davis

Bob Davis, who was born in Brawley, California but moved to Los Angeles when he was six, claims he grew up with the freeway system. His first instrument was the piano which he hated, so he took up the saxophone when he was twelve. By the time he was fourteen years old, he was playing with a band. He was asked to join the Lawrence Welk Orchestra in October of 1965 after he substituted for an absent musician, and stayed seventeen productive years.

Since the show went into retirement, Bob and his lovely wife, Sherry Aldridge, are living in Nashville, Tennesee, where he's working in country music clubs and recording session work. Bob heads up 17 musicians as a group called "Bob Davis and the Prime Time Orchestra." They recently completed a new big band album entitled "Turned-On Swing."

When asked about his future goals Bob said, "I intend to enjoy the rest of my life to the fullest of my capabilities and just to do more of the same. I love playing the saxophone too much to give it up."

Recipe for Remembrance

Bob says that the supreme highlight of his time on the show was meeting Sherry. "The other is that never before, and probably never again, will I have the opportunity to work with so many wonderful people."

Recipe

Bob is quite a cook. When we interviewed him, he was making a Caesar salad for dinner that night and shared his special recipe for the homemade croutons he puts in it. "I use seven grain bread and toast it in the toaster. The minute it comes out, I butter it and sprinkle it with garlic powder then cut it into cubes. Next, I harden it in the oven at 450 degrees, but you have to watch it closely so it won't burn." (We found that the croutons can also be hardened by slow baking them at 250 degrees for about one hour.)

The other recipe he gave us, Bob's Very Healthy Zucchini Soup, reflects the change in his eating habits in recent years. "Now that I'm older and considering the cholesterol scare and all of that, I refuse to eat gravies anymore. I eat very few desserts. We steam our vegetables and broil chicken and fish and that's about it."

BOB'S VERY HEALTHY ZUCCHINI SOUP

1 can chicken broth
1½ cups chopped zucchini
½ small onion, chopped
½ clove garlic, minced
2–3 handfuls spinach linguini (as much as you like)
½ cup soy sauce
¾ cup water

Combine the liquids in a pot. Bring to a boil, then add the remaining ingredients and simmer for 10 to 15 minutes.

Bob and Sherry

Ken Delo

Ken Delo was born and raised in Detroit, Michigan. He started performing at an early age for family and friends, entertaining them with impromptu magic shows, record pantomime, and plays he wrote. His singing career began when he was in high school and formed a vocal quartet. After graduating, Ken sang with several dance bands in the Detroit area and soon was appearing on local television shows. During a two year stint in the

Army, Ken performed throughout the thirteen state area of the Fifth Army.

After his discharge, Ken moved to Los Angeles to pursue his career. His very first audition landed him a job singing in a show at the world famous Hollywood Bowl, but subsequent singing and acting jobs led him from Alaska to Australia. His appearances on television and in supper clubs in the "land down under" were so well received that he made over one hundred television appearances and three specials of his own. He also wrote and starred in his own weekly television variety show. Doing this show, Ken was able to display his versatility as a host, interviewer, singer, actor, and comedian. The show won the annual "Logie" award (the equivalent of an Emmy) for best national variety show. He also hosted the game show "Name That Tune" five days a week.

Anxious to establish himself in his own country, he returned to the United States and began working in nightclubs, television, motion pictures, and doing legitimate stage. One of the programs he appeared on was The Lawrence Welk Show. After three guest appearances, Mr. Welk asked Ken to be a regular. For the next twelve years Ken had a busy career with the Musical Family.

Ken met his lovely wife Marilyn when they were performing in a show at the Veteran's Hospital in Dearborn, Michigan. They now live in the Los Angeles area with their daughter Kimberly, who is into tennis and singing, and their son, Kevin, who, according to his dad, lives and breathes baseball.

Like most other members of the Musical Family, Ken is continuing his career. He recently taped two shows for Group W Cable Television. He also writes. "I've got some scripts and other projects I'm hoping to sell and I wouldn't even mind producing. I have a little bit of everything stacked on my shelf: a horror movie, a comedy, a children's special." Recently, Ken has been asked to return to Australia to perform in one of that country's top variety shows. He is also negotiating for future specials of his own.

Recipe for Remembrance

"A major highlight was meeting a lot of the important people in show business. We guested top stars. Also, it was a thrill to play Madison Square Garden. I enjoyed being on a national television show that's viewed by 25 to 30 million people."

Recipes

These recipes, two of Ken's favorites, can be prepared ahead and are both tasty and easy to fix. We think you'll want to include them both on your menu the next time you entertain. For the Baked Stuffed Mushrooms Marilyn suggests that you use medium-sized mushrooms to serve as appetizers but use the giant ones if you plan to serve them as a main course.

BAKED STUFFED MUSHROOMS

¼ lb. Italian sausage (mild or hot)
1 cup chopped onions
1 lb. fresh mushrooms
¾ cup quick-cooking rice
¾ cup water
1 Tbsp. finely chopped parsley
1 tsp. salt
⅛ tsp. pepper
¾ cup mayonnaise
½ cup grated parmesan cheese

Remove the sausage from its casing and brown with the onion in a large skillet. Separate the stems from the mushrooms and chop fine. Add them to the meat mixture and brown lightly. Stir in the rice, water, parsley, and salt and pepper. Bring to a boil. Cover and remove from heat. Let stand for 5 minutes.

In a mixing bowl, combine the mayonnaise and cheese. Stir ½ cup into the rice mixture. Fill the mushrooms with the rice mixture. Place the stuffed mushrooms in a shallow baking dish. Top with the remaining cheese mixture and bake covered at 400 degrees for about 15 minutes or until the mushrooms are brown and puffy. Serve hot as either a luncheon entree or an appetizer.

BACON WRAPPED WATER CHESTNUTS

2 (8 ounce) cans water chestnuts, cut in half
bacon, cut into ⅓" or ¼" strips

Wrap the bacon around the chestnuts and secure with toothpicks. Bake for 30 minutes at 350 degrees. Drain the grease and add the sauce.

Sauce:
8 heaping Tbsp. brown sugar
1 (14 ounce) bottle catsup
1 Tbsp. lemon juice

Stir the sauce and pour it over the chestnuts. At this point you can refrigerate them until you are ready to serve them. Before serving, bake at 350 degrees for 30 minutes.

l. to r. Marilyn, Kevin, Kim and Ken

Ernest Ehrhardt

Ernest Ehrhardt, popular 'cellist on the Lawrence Welk Show for four years, has spent most of his career as a classical musician. He has played with Philharmonic Orchestras in Houston, Los Angeles, Buffalo, Tulsa, Long Beach, and Glendale, as well as being Principal 'Cellist for the American Ballet Theater, the Civic Light Opera, the Greek and Pantages Theaters, the Universal Amphitheater, and the Long Beach Grand Opera Association. He does numerous recordings for the film and recording industries and is currently on the faculty at Occidental College in Pasadena, California.

Recipes

Although Ernie doesn't cook, he is no stranger to good cuisine. His grandfather was chef to the Kaiser in Germany and his father managed many restaurants in the Los Angeles area, including Musso and Frank's in Hollywood. His Savory Savannah Squash can be served as a main dish or a side dish and can be prepared on the stovetop or in a microwave oven. Add a salad to accompany Ernie Ehrhardt's Great Aunt Mary's Rice Meatballs and you have a complete, nutritious, delectable meal.

SAVORY SAVANNAH SQUASH

1 small, finely chopped onion
2 medium fresh tomatoes, diced
garlic salt, to taste
leaf oregano, to taste (approximately 1 tsp.)
3 or 4 crookneck, yellow squash, diced
½ to 1 cup shredded Monterey jack cheese

In a medium sized skillet or saucepan, chop and brown the onion in a small amount of oil or butter. Add the diced tomatoes and brown lightly. Season with garlic salt and oregano, to taste. Add the diced squash. Cover and simmer on low until tender, about 20 to 25 minutes, or microwave at full power for 8 to 10 minutes. Add water if needed. When squash is tender, top it with Monterey jack cheese. Cover and simmer until the cheese melts (approximately another 5 minutes) or microwave at 50% power until cheese melts (about 2 minutes.)

ERNIE EHRHARDT'S GREAT AUNT MARY'S RICE MEATBALLS

1½ lbs. lean ground beef
1 onion, chopped
1 egg
3 Tbsp. dry parsley
dash of salt and pepper
1 cup water
1 Tbsp. sugar
1 (28 ounce) can stewed tomatoes
1 cup white, uncooked, long grain rice.

Combine the beef, onion, egg, rice and seasonings in a large bowl. Form into egg-sized meatballs. Combine the tomatoes, water and sugar in a large pot and bring to a rolling boil. Drop in the rice balls and simmer for approximately 1 hour. Serves 4–6.

Ralna English

Since the retirement of the Lawrence Welk Show, Ralna English has been sharing her great talent and beauty in main showrooms across the country, like Pittsburgh's Holiday House, The Blue Max in Chicago and Caesar's Palace in Atlantic City. Those illustrious settings are a far cry from Ralna's first "gig" with her junior high school rock 'n roll group in Lubbock, Texas. During those growing up years she was on a local television show called "Saturday Night Jamboree" and also traveled to little towns throughout Texas doing personal appearances on the back of a flatbed truck in town squares and on main streets. A Texas recording company soon spotted Ralna's terrific voice and signed her to a record contract that resulted in the release of "Fortune Teller," her first regional hit single.

During her college days at Texas Tech University, Ralna was chosen from among 1500 other hopefuls to star in a musical extravaganza at the Six Flags Over Texas Amusement Park. Following a move to Dallas, she was quickly singled out by a record company executive to sing commercial jingles. She says she snagged that job because, "I have this little child's voice that I use sometimes so I sang like a little kid who liked hamburgers."

Two years later Ralna was ready for the glitter of Hollywood. In no time, she was touring with Frank Sinatra, Jr., performing in a USO Tour to the Orient and appearing in Las Vegas and Lake Tahoe. When she wasn't on the road, Ralna performed with regulars such as Jim Nabors, Jack Jones, Vikki Carr and Steve Martin at the famous Santa Monica nightspot, The Horn. Her performances there led to her association with the Lawrence Welk Show.

She has also appeared on The Tonight Show, The Merv Griffin Show and The Mike Douglas Show. "Television is fun," Ralna admits, "but I love the live performances most." She tours regularly from coast to coast, appearing in showrooms and at state fairs. When she isn't center stage or in a recording studio, she enjoys relaxing with a good book or engaging in a game of tennis. Sometimes she participates in celebrity tennis tournaments.

Ralna and her singing partner, Guy Hovis, have sold more than five and one-half million albums. She is currently working on her first solo album much to the delight of her many loyal fans.

Recipe for Remembrance

Ralna enjoys giving back to people some of the blessings that have come her way. "Using the voice God gave me to make people happy has always been something that in turn has made me happy," Ralna confided. She is very active in her church and also in selected charities.

Recipe

Ralna is a true homebody who loves the simple life and especially covets the time she spends with her daughter, Julie. She's an excellent cook and was kind enough to share an old family favorite, Dang Good Pie.

DANG GOOD PIE

1 cube butter, softened
1½ cups sugar
2 Tbsp. flour
3 eggs
10 ounces crushed pineapple, drained
1 cup flaked coconut
½ tsp. vanilla
unbaked pieshell

Mix together softened butter, sugar and flour. Add eggs, one at a time, and mix well. Drain and add crushed pineapple, coconut and vanilla. Pour into unbaked pieshell and bake for 10 minutes at 450 degrees. Reduce heat to 350 degrees and bake until brown, or, as Ralna says, "Until it won't wiggle when you shake it."

♪Myron Floren ♪

When people think of Lawrence Welk the next person who pops into their minds is Myron Floren. His name is synonymous with the Musical Family. He is to Lawrence Welk what Tex Beneke was to Glenn Miller. Myron, who was assistant music director and an accordian player par excellence, joined the Lawrence Welk Orchestra in June of 1950. Lawrence discovered him when he was touring in St. Louis, Missouri, where

Myron was living at the time. "I had a night off so my wife, Berdyne, and I went down to the dance. Lawrence recognized me in the audience and asked me to come up and play the accordian. I saw him waving a white handkerchief from under the piano when I finished and he came over during intermission and offered me a job. I took it and that's how it all began."

A farmer's son, Myron was born and raised in South Dakota. He had rheumatic fever when he was in high school so he couldn't get into the regular armed forces during the war. Not wanting to shirk his patriotic duty, he volunteered for camp shows overseas service. "I had to sign a waiver releasing the Army from all responsibility or they wouldn't have let me go because I had a heart murmur. It wasn't like a club date. Sometimes we played six blocks from the front lines and did six to eight shows a day."

He met his wife, Berdyne, in Sioux Falls, South Dakota, when he was running an accordian studio at the Williams Piano Company. A salesman talked her parents into letting her take lessons. She didn't even want to take the accordian, she preferred piano, but she became one of her future husband's best students. They were married on August 19, 1945, when he got back from overseas. Over the years they have accumulated five daughters and four grandchildren.

Since the show went into retirement, Myron has continued doing about two hundred concerts a year alone and with members of the Musical Family. He is planning a pilot television show and hopes to bring the group back to the screen for a new series. "I think the music and entertainment business needs a Big Band Show with good, melodious music. You hear so many new shows coming on, and the videos, but nobody seems to know how to feature a big band. That's what I want to do." All in all, Myron says, "The future never looked brighter."

Recipe for Remembrance

Sorting out one special remembrance was difficult for Myron. There have been so many. "I remember a time when Alice Lon, who was the Champagne Lady at that time, and I played a date for a department store in San Diego. It was December and we flew down and back. As we were lining up to make our landing at Los Angeles International Airport, the pilot announced that the airport had just been closed due to heavy fog. We had a show we had to be on LIVE at 8:00 that evening, and this was happening around 6:00 P.M. We were rerouted to Burbank but, of course, my car was at LAX, so Alice and I took a taxi back there to get the car. Then, since I lived in Westchester, which is close to the airport, we stopped by my house and made a quick change. It was after 7:00 when we left for the studio. Normally, the trip from my place to the Aragon Ballroom took about twenty minutes but the fog was so heavy I got turned around and ended up going the wrong direction. We finally got to the ballroom just as the orchestra was playing the theme song. Lawrence didn't seem to be nervous. After the show I asked him if he wasn't worried when he saw that neither of us was there and he said, 'No. I knew you'd make it.'"

Myron also gave us his recipe for a happy marriage, which was originally printed in one of his concert programs. We were so taken with it, we asked his permission to include it. "My wife Berdyne and I have had a happy marriage for 37 years because we both learned what life is really about while we were growing up in South Dakota. As a child, I often saw a whole year of my parents' work and hopes wiped out when bad weather destroyed their crops. And Berdyne, who lived in the same farm area, experienced the same thing."

"When those disasters happened, my parents were sustained by keeping our family together and having great faith in God. And that's been the secret of our happy marriage. In bad times and good, our love of our home, our children, and our church gave us a stability that even a show biz career couldn't change."

"We were very young when we married—Berdyne was only 19 and I was 25—and we didn't have a dime. After I joined the Lawrence Welk Band in 1950, things brightened a lot for us. We had five baby girls in a row and I bought a big, comfortable house. When our children were young, Berdyne couldn't go on the road with me. But our faith in each other was so great she was never jealous of me when I was away, and I built up her self-confidence by calling every day to tell her what I was doing and to say 'I love you.'"

"Even though Berdyne and I have been married so many years, we still tell each other every day that we love each other—and we hug often. I feel that being married as long as we have doesn't mean that we should take each other for granted."

Recipes

Myron brags that his wife, Berdyne, is "the best cook in the world" and claims that four of his five daughters have followed in their mother's footsteps. The Pull Apart Herb Bread is a recipe from the kitchen of his daughter, Robin Floren Cipolla. Berdyne's Bean Dip is great to serve to crowds and can be made the day before.

BERDYNE'S BEAN DIP

1 (6 ounce) can bean dip
1 ripe avocado
1 tsp. lemon juice
1 cup sour cream
½ cup mayonnaise
1 pkg. taco seasoning mix
1 small, chopped onion
1 cup chopped black olives
2 large fresh tomatoes, finely diced

Spoon the bean dip into a dish. Mash the avocado then add the lemon juice and spread over the dip. Mix together the sour cream, mayonnaise and taco seasoning then add the onion, olives and tomatoes. Mix well then spread over the bean and avocado layer. Chill well. Serve with tortilla chips or corn chips.

PULL APART HERB BREAD

1 large package butterflake rolls
½ cup butter
1 Tbsp. parmesan cheese
1 tsp. chopped parsley
1 Tbsp. instant minced onion
¼ tsp. dill weed
garlic salt, to taste

Cut the rolls into bite-sized pieces. Melt the butter in a small saucepan then mix in the cheese, parsley, onions, dill and garlic salt. Toss the rolls lightly with one-half of the butter mixture. Arrange in a 9" square pan then pour the remaining butter mixture over the rolls and bake at 350 degrees for 15 minutes. (If you're in a hurry you can bake them at 450 degrees for 5–10 minutes.) Invert onto a serving plate.

Roselle Friedland

Many of you may never have seen or heard of Roselle Friedland, but you've enjoyed the fruit of her labor. Roselle was the women's hairdresser for the Lawrence Welk Show for eighteen years. She immigrated to the United States in 1954 from Frankfurt, Germany, and began her career working for Max Factor in Hollywood. From there she started doing local television shows and has beautified performers such as Carol Burnett, the Osmonds, and Sonny and Cher, as well as the stars and guests on the Lawrence Welk Show. Since the show went into retirement, Roselle is practicing her art in Hollywood and Las Vegas on stars like Toni Tenille, Tina Turner, Juliet Prowse, and Lynda Carter.

Recipe for Remembrance

During an interview at her Beverly Hills wig shop, Roselle chuckled and said, "I did the Carol Burnett Show for 11 years and Donny and Marie for 3 years. Between the host, guests and dancers I sometimes had 15, 25 or even 37 wigs to do for one show. On the Welk Show I got to work with real live hair."

Recipe

Roselle's contribution is an ethnic recipe from her homeland, Germany.

HAM AND CAULIFLOWER
1 head raw cauliflower
½ cup (1 cube) butter or margarine
3 Tbsp. flour
1 cup cold milk
salt and white pepper, to taste
dash nutmeg
2 drops soy sauce
20 strips pre-cooked ham (1″ thick x 4″ long)
2 cups grated Swiss cheese
Parmesan cheese

Steam or microcook the cauliflower until slightly underdone and still crunchy. Cool and break into flowerlets.

Sauce
Melt the butter over low heat, being careful not to brown. Stir in the flour. Slowly add the milk, a little at a time, stirring constantly to avoid lumps. Add the seasoning.

Cut the ham into strips, trimming off any fat. Arrange as follows in a 9″ x 13″ x 2″ baking dish. Spread a thin layer of sauce on the bottom of the dish. Arrange rows of cauliflowerlets, top with ham, and sprinkle evenly with Swiss cheese. Repeat until all ingredients are used. Pour the remaining sauce over the casserole, sprinkle with parmesan cheese and bake at 400 degrees for 1 hour or until the cheese bubbles. Serves 4–6.

Roselle and Rose with their staffs

Gail, Ron &
Michael

Gail, Ron and Michael are a trio of versatile, energetic performers whose vocal harmonies provide a wide range of sounds and styles. Their presentations include exciting renditions of Big Band era standards, contemporary up-tempo tunes and, their specialty: smooth, rich-blending ballads. As an act, the three were "new kids on the block" when they joined the Musical Family but their popularity was so immense that the trio received more mail than any other new group in the show's history.

Gail originated the idea of forming a mixed trio when she learned that the trio in which she was singing with Mary Lou Metzger and Sandi Griffiths was going to break up because Sandi was leaving the show. She'd been singing in trios since she was seven years old and didn't want to stop so she approached Lawrence with the concept. She didn't know what his reaction would be because until that time all of the groups had been formed using existing performers. This would be the first time in the history of the organization that a new act was created just for the show.

Mr. Welk liked Gail's suggestion. Ron thought auditioning for the show would be fun, so two-thirds of the trio was formed. When he asked Gail who she was going to get to round out the threesome, she said, "I don't know yet, but it will come to me." It did, one day when she was driving she remembered a talented musician she'd worked with on several other occasions—Michael Redman, Jr.

Michael originally met Gail through Tom Netherton. She phoned him and discussed the idea of putting together a mixed trio, stressing that this was a new and untried concept in the Musical Family. She asked him to meet with her and Ron to see if the three of them would hit if off both musically and personally. They did, so after they rehearsed for about two weeks, Gail arranged for an audition with Lawrence. They performed for him at his office on a rainy day in February at 7:30 in the morning. "Not exactly the most ideal time for singers," Michael noted.

They sang one of Mr. Welk's favorite songs, "And I Love You So." He told them, "I think that's the most beautiful blend I have ever heard in my life." Consequently, he arranged for them to audition for his staff. They were pleased with the close harmony and liked the idea that the trio was different from any other group on the show, but weren't sure there was room. The show had so many members already.

"Finally, they decided to give us a try, so our trio appeared early in the 1980 season and received such a great response from the audience that we were featured each week from then on," Michael explained.

Gail Farrell Anderson

Gail Farrell-Anderson was a regular performer on the Lawrence Welk Show for several seasons. An extremely versatile musician, Gail sang solo as well as in duos, trios and small groups, and played a variety of keyboard selections. Her piano artistry is an added feature of the

"Gail, Ron and Michael" trio's personal appearances.

Gail was born and raised in Durant, Oklahoma. "My family truly parallels a 'Grapes of Wrath' story," she shared. "A lot of my Mom's relatives were produce workers and my Dad was a cattle rancher."

Gail earned a bachelor's degree in classical piano at the University of Tulsa. Chosen Miss Tulsa, she won the talent and swimsuit competitions in the Miss Oklahoma pageant. Her sponsor from that event sent her to Los Angeles to train to be a Yamaha piano instructor. Her mother suggested, "While you're out there, why don't you try out for the Lawrence Welk Show?"

Gail decided to take her mother's advice. She contacted the vice-president of the Palladium, who suggested that she come down to the show one Saturday night and promised he'd try to get her on stage to sing for Mr. Welk. After sitting for what she felt was far too long, with no results, she decided to take matters into her own hands. When Lawrence came down into the audience to dance with some of the ladies, as was his custom, Gail tapped him on the shoulder and started dancing with him. She sang three songs on stage that night: "Downtown," "Cotton Fields," and "Sunny." That was enough to convince him that he should hire her. So she became a member of the Musical Family two weeks after graduating from college. Gail admits that, "At the time I didn't realize how lucky I was to have landed a steady job that would last all those years."

Although she was hired as a singer, it wasn't long before she was able to incorporate her other musical talents into her job, including playing the piano and arranging.

Gail has had no trouble keeping busy since the show retired. She has done numerous television commercials, performs with the trio and has just completed a French project — a record and music video which will run throughout Europe. She has her hands full as the proud mother of twins, Erin and Lauren, who were born in September of 1982.

Because of their "double duty," Ron and Gail try to stay as close to their Los Angeles home as possible and covet every moment they spend with their daughters.

Recipe for Remembrance

Gail has mused often about her good fortune at being hired so readily by such an illustrious organization. "I think Mr. Welk liked my philosophy. I believe in working hard and always trying to improve myself and that's central to his entire philosophy. I know I'm this way because I had a good upbringing in a fine family."

Recipes

Gail admitted that she doesn't cook fancy everyday but that she always wants any meal to be special, no matter how much work it takes. She gave us three mouth-wa-

tering recipes. Veal Piccata is a favorite that she's passed on to many other members of the Musical Family. Banana Ice Cream is a simple but showy dessert that's an appropriate ending to any meal or a great snack. Gail sometimes substitutes other fruit, such as berries or peaches, and suggests you experiment to find your favorite taste. The recipe for Mollie's Angel Food Pie came from her mother, Mollie Farrell. Gail says she's never known it to be served anywhere other than in her family. We found it was a delectable, delicious variation of an all-time favorite, angel food cake.

GAIL'S VEAL PICCATA

12 very thin fillets of veal
flour
¼ cup butter
¼ cup olive oil
½ cup dry white wine
3 Tbsp. parsley, chopped
1 Tbsp. fresh oregano, chopped OR ½ tsp.
    crushed oregano
1 Tbsp. fresh thyme, chopped OR 1 Tbsp.
    marjoram, finely chopped
salt and pepper
rind of 1 small lemon
lemon slices

Coat fillets with flour. Heat butter and olive oil in heavy frying pan. Sauté until golden brown, about 5 minutes. Remove from skillet and keep warm. Add wine to pan drippings and bring to simmer. Return veal to pan and add lemon rind, herbs and salt and pepper. Simmer 4 minutes. Serve topped with thin lemon slices. Serve with your favorite pasta side dish. Serves 4 to 6.

GAIL FARRELL'S BANANA ICE CREAM

5 eggs
2¼ cups sugar OR 1½ cup sugar plus ½ cup honey
    1 (13 ounce) can evaporated milk
1 (14 ounce) can sweetened, condensed
    milk
2 cups heavy cream
4 large, ripe bananas
3 Tbsp. vanilla extract
1½ quarts whole milk
1 package Knox gelatin
½ cup warm water
½ cup hot water

Dissolve gelatin in ½ cup warm water then stir in ½ cup hot water. Set aside. Pulverize bananas and sprinkle them with lemon juice to prevent discoloration. Beat eggs well in 8 quart mixing bowl. Gradually add remaining ingredients and stir. Freeze in a 2-gallon electric ice cream freezer for approximately 20 minutes or hand-crank until firm. Let stand in freezer compartment of refrigerator for 6 hours before serving. Makes 1½ gallons.

MOLLIE'S ANGEL FOOD PIE

1 baked, cooled 9 inch pieshell
1 cup fresh, sliced fruit (bananas, berries, peaches, etc.)

Filling
3 egg whites
pinch salt
⅓ cup sugar (for egg whites)
2 cups water
3 Tbsp. cornstarch, rounded
½ cup sugar
1 tsp. vanilla (optional) AND/OR
1 Tbsp. lemon juice (optional)

Beat egg whites with pinch of salt until stiff. Beat in ⅓ cup sugar. Set aside. Mix ½ cup sugar and cornstarch together in ½ cup cold water. Bring 1½ cups water to a boil. Gradually pour in cornstarch mixture, stirring constantly until transparent and thick. Gradually pour hot mixture into beaten egg whites, beating at medium speed using an electric mixer. Increase speed to high and beat for 10 minutes. Add vanilla and/or lemon juice, if desired.

Topping
1 cup whipping cream
4–6 Tbsp. powdered sugar
¼ tsp. vanilla (optional) AND/OR
1 tsp. lemon juice (optional)

Whip cream until stiff, adding sugar and flavorings while beating. Cover bottom of pieshell with fruit. Cover fruit with filling. Add whipped cream topping. Garnish with fruit or top with chopped nuts if using bananas. Chill for 1 hour or until ready to serve.

Lauren and Erin

Ron Anderson

Baritone Ron Anderson was born and raised in San Francisco. He has a broad background in both entertainment and business and says he has always considered himself an instrumentalist rather than a vocalist. He started playing the trombone when he was twelve years old and music has been an integral part of his life since that time.

Ron, who majored in music history, literature and conducting, attended

Bethany College in Santa Cruz, California. When he wasn't in the classroom, he was performing throughout the United States and Canada. During his senior year, he was hired as choir director by a large church in Oakland. While attending graduate school at California State University in Hayward, he produced the music for a weekly television broadcast. Later he was employed as music director of a church in San Jose for five years.

In 1973 Ron uprooted from Northern California and headed for Los Angeles. He took a job in real estate but was still performing the entire time, in a gospel brass quartet. After he relocated to Southern California, Ron expanded his show business career. Starting as a stand-in actor for game show hosts during rehearsal, he soon secured bit parts which led to other acting jobs, such as appearances on The Mary Tyler Moore Show, The Young and the Restless, The Tonight Show and various film and stage productions. Ron still records, occasionally acts as a substitute host on game shows, and also produces educational video tapes. He is currently expanding his production efforts to include game shows, variety and other show business ventures.

Ron met Gail in an acting workshop class in 1977 and they were married two years later. He says, "My idea of a vacation is being at home with Gail and the twins."

Recipe for Remembrance

Ron reminisced about his conception of the Musical Family. "It really was, in the truest sense of the word, a family. Some people on the show worked together for over thirty years. They went through marriages, children growing up and getting married, deaths. They were truly a family, and when Michael and I joined the group we were welcomed like relatives who belonged but hadn't lived in the area for a while."

Recipes

Ron contributed three fabulous recipes to our culinary collection. The Anderson children always loved Crumby Chicken, which

Lauren and Erin

got its name when Ron's mother once asked, "What would you kids like for dinner tonight?" and his sister, Sharon, replied, "Fix crumby chicken."

Ron's and Gail's dinner guests always look forward to drinking his fabulous Cranberry Slush. It cools hot brows in the summertime and is a perfect beverage to serve at Thanksgiving and Christmas holiday parties and meals. The Crab Mold, which he personally hates, always receives rave reviews and is a favorite hor d'oeuvre among members of the Musical Family. Gail likes to serve it with Wheatsworth Crackers.

CRUMBY CHICKEN

8 chicken breasts, skinned
½ cup melted butter
1 clove garlic, finely chopped OR ¼ tsp. garlic powder
1 cup cornflakes
1 cup potato chips

"Smush" (that's how they do it at the Anderson household) cornflakes and potato chips into tiny pieces with a rolling pin then place in a pie tin and set aside. Melt butter with garlic. Dip chicken breasts in melted butter then roll in crumbs until thoroughly covered. Bake at 350 degrees for 1 hour. Serves 4 to 8, depending on appetites.

RON'S CRANBERRY SLUSH

1 can frozen, undiluted cranberry juice cocktail
1 banana
1 heaping Tbsp. coconut snow
1 can club soda OR ⅔ cup vodka
12–16 ice cubes

Blend in blender at high speed until smooth and slushy. If necessary, add ice cubes to achieve proper consistency.

RON'S CRAB MOLD

1 envelope unflavored gelatin
1 (10¾ ounce can) undiluted cream of mushroom soup
1 (8 ounce) package cream cheese
8 ounces fresh crab OR 1 (7½ ounce) can crabmeat, drained
½ cup mayonnaise
½ cup sour cream
2 Tbsp. parsley, minced or flakes
1 cup finely chopped celery
4 green onions, finely chopped
dash pepper
⅛ cup lemon juice OR ¼ cup white wine

Heat mushroom soup in double boiler. Add cream cheese and stir until smooth. Remove from heat. Add crab, mayonnaise, sour cream, parsley, celery and onion. Dissolve gelatin in 3 Tbsp. cold water and add to crab mixture. Add wine OR lemon juice. Spray mold with Pam, add crab mixture and refrigerate overnight. Serves 10 to 12.

Jonathan Anderson

Grant Anderson

Michael Redman, Jr.

Michael Redman, Jr., tenor in the popular trio of Gail, Ron, and Michael, is originally from Portland, Oregon. Always a performer at heart, immediately after graduating from the University of Southern California in Los Angeles, with a degree in Performing Arts and

Languages, Michael started working in the entertainment industry.

As a vocalist, he has performed and recorded with notables like Frank Sinatra, Barbra Streisand, Barry Manilow, The Carpenters, Bobby Vinton, Elvis Presley, Florence Henderson, Henry Mancini, and Kenny Rogers. Michael's television credits include Happy Days, Laverne and Shirley, Donny and Marie, Sonny and Cher, Bob Hope, the Tonight Show, Carol Burnett, Perry Como, John Davidson, Eight is Enough, and Merv Griffin, as well as the Emmy and Academy Award Shows. Michael currently appears in various television and radio commercials including Hallmark, Levi's, Kellogg's, Chevrolet, 7-Up, Honda, VISA, and Ford. His film credits include Urban Cowboy, House Calls, Poseidon Adventure, Blues Brothers, Lady Sings the Blues, Annie, Apocalypse Now, Elvis: Life Story, Oh, God, and Oh God, Book II and Oh God, You Devil.

Michael has been extremely busy since the show retired. "I'm preparing to co-star in a situation comedy television show in New Zealand, where I did the pilot last year. The show, which is called 'The Cleaning Company,' has been sold world-wide. I'm the only American in the story so far. My family will be going with me when I go to New Zealand to tape the show."

Michael and Cinda

Michael also writes television scripts and screenplays. He has done two solo albums and one with the trio, called "Joyful Noise." He and his wife, Cinda, who is one of the co-authors of this book, often do concerts together. She plays classical piano and accompanies him. They met when they were attending the University of Southern California. They were married in 1968. Although they live in the San Fernando Valley, with their daughters Jennifer Kathryn and Melissa Hope, they like to spend as much time as possible in the Pacific Northwest.

"To me, that's God's country," Michael mused. "I feel privileged to be in Los Angeles and to be part of the entertainment industry, and to have had an exciting and fulfilling career, but my heart still remains up there. I like to get up to our lake home as often as possible. It's located forty-five minutes from Portland, just off the Columbia River on the Washington side. It's a little bit of heaven for us, an escape from the fast, crazy pace of Hollywood, a chance to fish, swim, boat, and walk through the evergreen trees and ferns."

Michael's future plan is to continue his entertainment career. He also has a career in the Gospel field, which he looks on as a ministry. "I like to share with audiences the goodness of the Lord and the way God has blessed our family. I try to encourage others to look to their Heavenly Father as a source of fulfillment and happiness in their lives."

Recipe for Remembrance

"Being part of a television musical era in American history was a unique privilege. I love television and I love performing for audiences—especially a large, appreciative one like the Welk show audience always has been. It was an honor to be part of the music that was presented to them for so many years. It was fun, too, to be part of a new Musical Family. I gained a lot of new friends."

Recipes

Every Sunday morning before church, Michael prepares a breakfast of pancakes or waffles, sausage, and fresh fruit for the family. He likes to cook and smoke fish, but

beyond that he leaves the culinary chores to Cinda.

She recalled a slight disaster that convinced her that was the best arrangement. "When we were dating in college Michael cooked a couple of unmentionable dinners. One was a pork chop recipe that involved curry. In his infinite wisdom, he thought if a little was good, a lot would be better, so added about 3 tablespoonfuls. There was so much curry it discolored the Teflon spatula."

"Another time, he fixed a game hen. He followed most of the directions. He washed it carefully and rubbed it with the proper spices, but he forgot to clean out the inside. It tasted awful and smelled even worse. That's when he decided he'd leave the cooking to me."

Michael contributed four of his favorite recipes. Michael's grandmother, Janet Farley Janes, always made the Zucchini Bread for her grandson when he visited her in her home in the San Francisco Bay area. Mrs. Janes, who passed away two weeks before Michael auditioned for the show, claimed that if she didn't watch him carefully, he would eat all eight miniature loaves before anyone else could sneak a bite. Michael says to be sure the bread isn't overbaked and that it's especially tantalizing when served hot from the oven.

Michael, Jennifer, Melissa and Cinda

Melissa and Jennifer

3 tsp. vanilla
2 cups fresh, raw zucchini squash
3 cups flour
1 tsp. salt
½ tsp. baking powder
1 tsp. baking soda
3 tsp. cinnamon
1 cup chopped nuts, optional

Blend eggs, oil, sugars, vanilla and zucchini slices in a blender until well mixed. Add the cinnamon, salt, baking powder, baking soda, and blend until mixed. Pour into a large bowl and add the flour. Add chopped nuts last, if desired. Divide the batter equally into eight miniature loaf pans that have been greased with a vegetable shortening spray. Bake for 1 hour at 350 degrees.

Mrs. Janes' Grasshopper Pie is another favorite at the Redman house. It's much lighter on the creme de menthe than most. Cinda said, "We always chuckled about how Grandma could never bring herself to enter a liquor store to buy the creme de menthe and creme de cocoa. She'd always enlist someone else to purchase it for her."

The recipe for Artichoke Bits comes from Cinda's mother, Kay Goold, who lives in Sacramento, California. It's extremely rich but yummy delicious. It's a party favorite at the Redman's.

Cinda's sister Pat Flug, who lives in Aspen, Colorado, contributed the More Than Just A Salad Dressing recipe. Cinda serves it on the side to spoon over salmon, pours it over steamed broccoli, and uses it as a dip for cold artichokes. She suggests that you vary the amount of mayonnaise and mustard if you want it thicker.

GRASSHOPPER PIE

Crust
16 Hydrox or Oreo cookies
5 Tbsp. melted butter
Crush cookies, mix with butter, and press firmly into a 9″ glass pie plate.
Filling
⅔ cup milk
24 marshmallows
½ pint whipping cream
1½ jiggers creme de menthe
½ jigger white creme de cocoa
(jigger = ⅛ cup)
In a double boiler, combine the milk and marshmallows and heat until dissolved. Set aside to cool. Whip the cream and fold into the liqueurs. Fold into cooled marshmallow mixture. Mix and pour into crust. Refrigerate until firm.

ZUCCHINI BREAD

3 eggs
1 cup salad oil
2 cups sugar
½ cup brown sugar

MORE THAN A JUST A SALAD DRESSING

¼ tsp. salt
¼ tsp. pepper
¼ tsp. garlic powder
½ tsp. dijon mustard
1 Tbsp. mayonnaise
2 Tbsp. lemon juice
7 Tbsp. olive oil

Shake well or blend in blender until well mixed. Chill and serve.

ARTICHOKE BITS

2 (6 ounce) jars artichoke hearts
½ cup onion, finely chopped
2 cloves garlic, minced or mashed
4 large eggs
¼ cup dried, fine bread crumbs
¼ tsp. salt
⅛ tsp. pepper
⅛ tsp. oregano
large pinch thyme
large pinch sage
¼ tsp. Tabasco sauce

2 Tbsp. parsley, chopped
½ lb. sharp cheddar cheese, grated

Drain marinade from 1 jar of artichokes into a frying pan. (Discard the rest.) Chop artichoke hearts and set aside. Add the onions and garlic to the marinade and sauté until limp but not brown. Remove from heat. Beat eggs. Stir in the bread crumbs and seasonings. Add all remaining ingredients and mix well. Pour into an 8" square pan, sprinkle with thyme and bake at 325 degrees for 30 minutes.

Melissa and Jennifer

Clay & Sally Hart

The dynamic performing duo, Clay and Sally Hart, have been entertaining audiences throughout the country and gaining further national acclaim since they left the Lawrence Welk show in the mid-seventies. Sally Flynn, a slender, dark-haired beauty from Ontario, Oregon, came to the Musical Family with her singing partner, Sandi Griffiths, in 1967. Sally and Sandi had been appearing with performers like Jack Jones and Joey Bishop when Lawrence auditioned them. They won the place vacated by the Lennon Sisters and went on to become one of the most popular acts in the history of the show. Sally has appeared on several national television commercials and programs and recently released her first chart record, "Take What I Can Get."

Clay Hart hails from Providence, Rhode Island. He was hired on the spot by Lawrence Welk in 1968 when the maestro heard him sing in Charleston, West Virginia. Clay filled the country music spot vacated by Lynn Anderson. His great pop-country style was an immediate hit with both Mr. Welk and country music fans. Clay's first record, "Spring," won him a Grammy nomination as best country male vocalist of the year. He has been featured on the Grand Ole Opry and in several national television commercials.

The Harts met on the show and started dating in 1970. In 1973, Sally left the show to appear in clubs and do commercials. They were married in 1974 and the following year, Clay also left the show. Sally mused, "Clay hired me to go out on the road as part of his show. It was the best decision we could have made because it meant we could be together."

Clay and Sally have blended their individual talents into an energetic contemporary and country musical experience. Their growing list of credits includes performing as the opening act for Red Skelton, Alan King, Barbara Mandrell, T. G. Sheppard, The Statler Brothers and Juliet Prowse. They keep busy headlining many of the country's major regional and county fairs, as well as performing for numerous conventions for major business corporations throughout the United States.

Recipe for Remembrance

When we caught up with Clay and Sally they were on one of their many nationwide tours. Sally reminisced about the many lessons she learned from her association with Lawrence Welk. "Clay has the same kind of professionalism as Lawrence and it really changed my life. We were taught always to be on time for our job, to take care of the people who hired us, to give an extra moment for autographs and to be appreciative to the audience for coming to see us. Clay has always been this way but I was very young when I started performing and I didn't think of those things."

Clay and Sally have fond memories of their time with the Musical Family and both say they miss the wonderful comradery with the performers on the show.

Recipes

Clay and Sally travel so much they don't spend a lot of time in the kitchen but when they are at home in Nashville, Tennessee, they both enjoy contributing their talents to preparing meals. Sally donated two tasty delights from her mother, Norma Jesse Flynn, who lives in Desert Hot Springs, California. Quick Cottage Cheese Salad is easy to prepare and the Cranberry Salad can be a special treat for holiday tables or complements everyday fare equally well.

Clay's Classic Hollandaise Sauce evolved when he experimented until he found just the taste he liked. Clay recommends using the sauce as a meat dip or with artichokes, as well as in a traditional manner on vegetables or eggs.

QUICK COTTAGE CHEESE SALAD

1 pint small curd cottage cheese
2 Tbsp. mayonnaise
1 (8 ounce) can crushed pineapple, drained
2 cups miniature marshmallows
½ pint whipping cream, whipped and sweetened to taste
½ cup nuts, chopped

Mix together and chill well. Serves 4 to 6.

CRANBERRY SALAD

1 pound fresh cranberries
1½ cups sugar
16 marshmallows, cut into quarters
3 red delicious apples, diced
1 cup celery, diced
1 cup nuts, chopped
½ pint whipping cream

Grind cranberries. Add sugar and let stand in refrigerator overnight. Three hours before serving, add marshmallows, apples, celery and nuts. Stir well and let stand in refrigerator. One hour before serving, whip cream and add to cranberry mixture. Chill and serve. Serves 6 to 8.

CLAY'S CLASSIC HOLLANDAISE SAUCE

½ cube (4 Tbsp.) butter
2 Tbsp. mayonnaise
½ tsp. dry mustard
juice from ½ fresh lemon
1 Tbsp. parmesan cheese
garlic salt
1 egg yolk
2 Tbsp. milk

Melt butter over low heat. Add mayonnaise, mustard, lemon juice, parmesan cheese and egg yolk. Stir over very low heat while adding garlic salt to taste. Add milk and stir until sauce is proper consistency.

Bob Havens

Bob Havens, who was trombonist with the Lawrence Welk Orchestra for twenty-two years, started his musical career at the age of five in his hometown of Quincy, Illinois, playing violin. When he was about eight years old he took up the trombone and piano but somewhere along the way decided he liked trombone best.

After attending one semester at Culver-Stockton College in Canton, Missouri, he moved to New Orleans and eventually played Dixieland music with Al Hirt's band and became friends with both Al Hirt and Pete Fountain. In 1960 he received a call from Lawrence Welk asking him to join the show. "It was quite an opportunity. I was very happy in New Orleans but it really didn't present an all-around exposure to music so I made the move."

When asked what his plans are for the future Bob reflected, "In a way, when Mr. Welk retired, I guess you could say the rest of the band retired too, at least from doing a regular television show. Now each one of us would be classified as free-lance musicians. I hope in the future to continue doing more in the jazz field because I'm really a jazz musician."

Currently, Bob is doing guest appearances with jazz bands around the country and playing in jazz concerts and at festivals.

Bob and his wife, Connie, who were married in 1976, met when he was touring with the Lawrence Welk band in 1974. After a performance in Providence, Rhode Island, a lady and her daughter (Connie and her mother) asked for his autograph. Bob says, "I happened to run into them later at the hotel where we were staying so I invited them for cocktails. At that point I was interested in visiting with them because I found out that Connie's mother was from my home town and had gone to school there." But, he confesses, "All the time I was getting acquainted with her mother, I had my eye on Connie. We ended up writing letters to each other and had a relationship by mail. Eventually, we got married."

Now, Bob and Connie are the proud parents of a son, Robby, and a daughter, Kari Lynn.

Recipe for Remembrance

For those of you who think show business is all glamour and romance, Bob shared this story. "I recall a time when we were on tour and had to fly from Little Rock, Arkansas, to Dallas, Texas during a terrible storm. When we arrived in Dallas there was a tornado alert in effect. It was so foggy you couldn't see anything. We circled the field for almost an hour and finally the weather was so bad we had to go back to Little Rock. The flight was so bumpy that practically everyone in the band was saying their prayers because we had the feeling we weren't going to make it. After we landed, the pilot happened to mention to one of the people in the band that during the time we were circling the field in Dallas the control tower operators were alerted about the tornado and left their posts. There wasn't even a radar signal and they had about twenty planes circling the field with no control. We barely missed hitting another plane by about ten feet!"

Bob, Connie, Kari Lynn and Robby

Recipe

Bob reached back into the past and shared a favorite recipe he collected in New Orleans many years ago. He told us, "Red Beans and Rice is a New Orleans dish. You usually cook it with a special creole spice and crab oil. We've never been able to find that here." We found that, even minus the spice and crab oil, served with cole slaw, the rice and beans makes a complete, nutritious meal. It can be cooked according to Bob's instructions or slow-cooked in a crockpot for 8 to 10 hours without pre-soaking the beans.

RED BEANS AND RICE

2 cups (1 lb.) dried red kidney beans
2½ quarts water
5 strips bacon, cut into 1″ pieces
   (substitute ham hock or ¼ lb. salt pork
   if preferred)
1 pod garlic (or ¼ tsp. garlic powder)
salt and pepper to taste
uncooked rice

Soak beans overnight in 1 quart water. Add another 1½ quarts. Add the bacon (or other meat), garlic, and a pinch of salt. Simmer slowly 3 to 4 hours, or until the beans are very soft and the water has cooked down to make a thick, red sauce. Salt and pepper to taste then serve over rice, which has been prepared according to package directions. Serves 4.

Arthur "Skeets" Herfurt

When Skeets Herfurt was nine years old, his music-loving dad
spotted a shiny soprano saxophone in a show window and on a
whim bought it for his son. It was a gift that set the entire course of his life.

Skeets has been in love with music ever since. Over fifty years ago, when he was attending the University of Denver, he and his student band were booked into the Broadmoor Country Club in Denver and were enjoying considerable popularity. They had to scurry for another spot when the owner informed them they were being replaced by a new band that was coming in from North Dakota—Lawrence Welk and his Hotsy Totsy Band.

Five decades after being bumped out of an assignment by Lawrence Welk, Skeets joined the Musical Family as its star saxophonist. Who says it isn't a small world?

After his unexpected departure from the Broadmoor Country Club, Skeets had little trouble finding other engagements with famous bands like Tommy and Jimmy Dorsey, Nelson Riddle, Frank DeVol, Paul Weston, Alvino Rey, Ray Noble and Georgia Stoll. Eventually he went to New York with Glenn Miller where they both joined the newly-formed Dorsey Brothers Orchestra. Later, Skeets segued with Bing Crosby to the West Coast to do the Kraft Music Hall and was much in demand by music recording groups for radio and television shows, including "My Three Sons," "The Danny Thomas Show," and "The Dick Van Dyke Show." Frank Sinatra, Red Skelton and Danny Kaye are among the many who have relied on his expert sax work.

Skeets has been married for almost thirty years to Dorothy Brillhart of Los Angeles, who is a noted Bible lecturer and graduate of Goddard College in Vermont. They met at a church in Beverly Hills. "On our first date, Skeets took me to the Beverly Hills Hotel for dinner and dancing," Dorothy laughs. "I was amazed when, during the breaks, the entire band surrounded our table and I was immediately lost in a world of musical language throughout the evening! But today, I can speak that language with the best of them."

Finally retired, Skeets says his loftiest goal for the future is, "to have my artichokes grow bigger and my avocadoes grow and produce and for my fruit trees to bear fruit. I just want to grow the produce of the land."

Recipe for Remembrance

"I think it's your love for what you're doing that gets through to an audience. To me, Mr. Welk is the personification of that love: his love of music, of entertaining people, the way he talks to the audiences and the way they respond totally to him."

Recipes

When asked if he cooks, Skeets said. "I used to, but I gave it up because I have two beautiful angels in my kitchen who do it for me." Those angels are his wife and her sister, who came to live with the Herfurts when her husband passed away.

Skeets gave us four of his favorite recipes. Herfurt Hamburger Soup has been in his family for years. Skeets says the Stuffed Flank Steak With Dressing is one his friends like to have served when they come over. Pumpkin Chiffon Pie and French Mousse Chantilly are always a tremendous hit.

PUMPKIN CHIFFON PIE

Soak 1 Tbsp. gelatine in ¼ cup cold water. Beat slightly 3 egg yolks.

Add:

½ cup sugar
1¼ cups canned or fresh cooked pumpkin
½ cup milk
¼ tsp. salt
½ tsp. cinnamon
½ tsp. nutmeg

Cook and stir ingredients in double boiler until thick. Stir in soaked gelatine until it is dissolved. Set aside and chill. Whip until stiff 3 egg whites with ¼ tsp. salt. When the pumpkin mixture begins to set, stir in ½ cup sugar and fold in the egg whites. Fill either a baked pie shell or graham cracker crust. Chill the pie for several hours. Top with whipped cream.

FRENCH MOUSSE CHANTILLY

1 cup milk
2 ounces unsweetened chocolate
1½ tsp. unflavored gelatin
1 cup whipped cream
½ cup sugar
1 tsp. vanilla

Heat milk and chocolate over medium heat until chocolate melts. Blend until smooth. Blend gelatin and sugar and add to chocolate, stirring constantly to dissolve. Chill until slightly thickened. Add vanilla. Fold in whipped cream. Spoon into Demitasse Cups. Chill. Makes 6 servings.

HERFURT HAMBURGER SOUP

3 Tbsp. butter
1 medium onion, coarsely chopped
1½ lbs. lean ground beef
3½ cups canned or stewed tomatoes
3 (10½ ounce) cans consomme
2 cans water
4 medium carrots, quartered
1 bay leaf
4 celery tops, chopped
6 sprigs parsley
½ tsp. thyme
10 peppercorns
1 Tbsp. salt

Cook onion in melted butter until limp. Add beef and cook until the red color is gone. Add remaining ingredients. Cover and simmer over low heat for one hour. Cool. Skim off fat. Reheat and serve. Serves 6.

STUFFED FLANK STEAK WITH DRESSING

1 (2 to 3 lb.) flank steak
1 tsp. salt
⅛ tsp. paprika

Tenderize steak, using either a commercial tenderizer or by pounding with a kitchen mallet. Sprinkle meat with salt and paprika. Set aside and make the stuffing.

Stuffing

¼ cup butter
2 Tbsp. chopped onion
1 lb. ground veal
1 cup bread crumbs
¼ tsp. salt
dash paprika
2 Tbsp. chopped parsley
3 Tbsp. chopped celery
1 egg, slightly beaten

In a large skillet, sauté the onion in butter until brown. Add the veal and brown slightly. Add bread crumbs, salt, paprika, parsley, celery and egg. Mix well and spread over the steak. Roll loosely and tie. Sear in hot oil on all sides until nicely browned. Top with sauce then bake in a tightly covered pan at 250 degrees for 1½ hours or until tender.

Sauce

1 cup tomato juice OR 1 cup beef consomme
¼ tsp. salt
1¼ Tbsp. flour

Mix flour and salt into liquid. Pour over steak. Serves 4–6.

Laroon Holt

Laroon Holt, whose talented trumpeteering delighted Lawrence Welk fans for nine and one-half years, has always belonged to a "musical" family. His father, who was a farmer in Barnes, Kansas, played the trumpet and his mother and two sisters also played instruments.

While attending the Conservatory of Music in Kansas City, Missouri, Laroon played with the Kansas City Philharmonic Orchestra. After graduating, he traveled with Warren Covington, leader of the Tommy Dorsey Orchestra. After moving to Los Angeles in 1962, he worked various nightclubs, television shows, and recording sessions with such illustrious greats as Les Brown, Ray Anthony, Stan Kenton, Tex Beneke, and Nelson Riddle.

Laroon and his wife, Claudine, make their home in Pasadena, California, and have two college-age children, Tim and Heidi.

Recipe for Remembrance

Laroon playfully said "I do not cook anything more serious than a steak or oatmeal. I like the simple things: meat, vegetables, salad and ice cream." Laroon added, "The more I eat, the more I exercise! A wonderful combination, I believe."

Recipe

Laroon contributed a delicious Pepper Steak to our culinary collection. "This is a little dish I enjoy. Claudine puts it together, not me! I never got past 'simple' in cooking." It's a perfect, quick and easy microwave dish that looks and tastes like you've spent all day preparing it. He suggests that the steak is easier to slice if it is partially frozen.

LAROON HOLT'S PEPPER STEAK

1½ lb. boneless, beef round steak
1 Tbsp. olive oil
1 clove minced garlic
3 medium green or red peppers (or combination), seeded and sliced into thin strips
1 large, peeled, fresh tomato, seeded and cut into strips
¾ cup beef bouillon
¼ cup soy sauce
1¼ tsp. ground ginger
¼ tsp. sugar
pepper to taste
3 Tbsp. cornstarch
cooked rice

Cut the beef diagonally into 2" x ½" strips. Microwave the oil on high in a 3 quart casserole for 1 minute. Stir in the beef and garlic and microwave on high for 4 minutes, stirring twice, or until the meat is lightly browned. Stir in the peppers and tomatoes and microwave on full power for 3 minutes. Stir in the soy sauce, ginger, sugar, pepper, and half of the beef bouillon. Cover and microwave on high for 6 to 8 minutes, until the meat is fork tender. Stir the cornstarch into the remaining beef broth and add it to the meat mixture. Microwave on high for 4 minutes, stirring twice, until the sauce thickens. Remove from the oven. Let stand covered for 10 to 15 minutes. Serve on a bed of cooked rice. Serves 4.

Larry Hooper

Larry Hooper was born in Lebanon, Missouri. He joined the Welk organization in 1948 as a piano player. He and the late Jerry Burke often entertained with their "twin" pianos. In 1952 his deep bass singing voice was unearthed when he recorded the hit song, "Oh, Happy Day." This led to many other favorites, such as "Minnie the Mermaid," "Big John," and "Grandfather's Clock." On the show, Larry was also featured in barber shop

71

quartet numbers. He was one of the most popular and admired members of the Musical Family, both by the audience and his fellow performers.

Larry and his lovely wife, Beverly, were married in 1952 and had three lovely daughters; Lori, Melinda, and Lisa, and one granddaughter, Jolene. His hobby was model railroads and he boasted many collector's items in his collection. He and his family spent the last twenty years of their lives in La Crescenta, California. He passed away in June of 1983 after a long illness. We are extremely pleased to be able to include him in **RECIPES FOR REMEMBRANCE.** Lawrence Welk fans will never forget Larry or the pleasure his beautiful music brought them.

Recipes

Mrs. Hooper contributed two recipes that were among her husband's favorites.

CARROT CAKE MUFFINS
In blender or food processor combine:
3 cups grated carrots
1½ cups salad oil
4 eggs
In mixing bowl combine:
2 cups whole wheat flour
2 cups brown sugar
1 cup bran flakes
1½ tsp. baking soda
2 tsp. cinnamon
¼ tsp. nutmeg
¼ tsp. allspice

Combine all ingredients and pour into well-greased muffin tins. Bake at 375 degrees for 23 minutes. Makes 30 muffins.

Larry and Mary Lou

BEST BAKED FISH
1 lb. red snapper or other fillets
1 Tbsp. butter
1 small onion, chopped
dash of garlic powder
1 green onion, chopped
¼ cup dry white wine
pinch of thyme and basil
3 ounces vegetable or tomato juice
1 (6 ounce) can tomato sauce
1 cup Monterey Jack cheese, grated

Sauté onions and garlic in melted butter. Add all other ingredients except fish. Simmer 10 minutes. Cut fillets into serving size pieces and place in 9" x 13" x 2" baking dish. Top with sauce and grated cheese. Bake for 30 minutes at 350 degrees. Serves 4 to 6.

Guy Hovis

Handsome Guy Hovis is a native of Tupelo, Mississippi. After high school, Guy attended the University of Mississippi where he received a degree in accounting. After a few months as an accountant apprentice, he spent two years as an Artillery Lieutenant in the United States Army. After his discharge, he returned to graduate school but left after one semester to follow a dream.

Guy had been singing all of his life and had always hoped to give show business a try. So, one day he simply piled all of his belongings into his car and headed for California. Guy remembers, "I was going to give myself one summer to make it or break it. The first thing I did when I got to Los Angeles was head for The Horn, a nightclub in Santa Monica. I had heard so much about it from my friend, Tom Lester, who played Eb on the television show, 'Green Acres.' I used to sing at The Horn late at night when they ran out of performers."

Even though Guy had parts in three musicals at the Valley Music Theater, he was about ready to pack up and go back to Mississippi when the producer of Art Linkletter's "House Party" saw him perform and asked him to appear on that show. He did thirteen "House Party" programs in three months and during that time says he was "fatally bitten by the show biz bug." Guy's stint on "House Party" led to appearances on other television shows, such as NBC Showcase, Donald O'Connor and the Joey Bishop Show. He also recorded an album.

In spite of these early successes, Guy says that his career didn't really get off the ground until he joined Ralna as a guest on the 1969 Lawrence Welk Christmas Show. They rapidly became one of the most popular Musical Family acts since the Lennon Sisters. They have been seen on many television variety and game shows and their personal appearances around the country are always sell outs.

Guy is currently writing and producing a revue for the theater at the Lawrence Welk Village in Escondido, CA. He will also appear in the revue.

Recipe for Remembrance

Raised on hymns and gospel music, Guy said, "I was singing solos in church when I was five years old. In high school I sang for weddings and at civic functions but didn't consider a career in music until many years later when, at the urging of some of my Army buddies, I entered my first talent contest—and won! I ended up doing a six week tour with the Fourth Army and loved it." That was only the beginning of what would become a full and busy show business career.

Recipe

Sharing a simple but favorite recipe of his mother's, Francis Hovis of Tupelo, Mississippi, Guy told us, "This Broccoli Casserole is a delicious dish she's been making for the family for years." If you're from the South, he recommends using sweet milk in place of regular milk.

BROCCOLI CASSEROLE

2 cups cooked rice
1 (10 ounce) package frozen, chopped
    broccoli
1/3 cup Kraft Cheese Whiz
1 (10¾ ounce) can cream of chicken soup,
    undiluted
1 (6 ounce) can water chestnuts, chopped

½ cup celery, chopped
¼ cup onion, chopped
3 Tbsp. butter or margarine
½ cup milk

Cook and drain broccoli. Cook rice accord-
ing to package instructions. Sauté chopped
celery and onion in melted butter for about
5 minutes. In a separate saucepan, heat the
cream of chicken soup, milk and Cheese
Whiz until the cheese is melted. Add
sautéed celery, onions, water chestnuts, rice
and broccoli to the soup mixture. Blend
well and bake in a 2-quart casserole at 350
degrees for 30–40 minutes. Serves 4.

Paul Humphrey

From the time he started taking drum lessons when he was six years old, Paul Humphrey knew he wanted to be a professional musician. Although he has played other instruments, drums were always number one with him. By the time he joined the Lawrence Welk Band in 1976 he had been a musician for most of his life and widely regarded as one of the best drummers in the Los Angeles recording industry.

Since the show's retirement Paul is continuing his work as a studio musician, as well as performing at jazz festivals, writing music instruction books for drum, and maintaining his own jazz group, the Paul Humphrey Sextet. He was drummer for the hit musical "Sophisticated Ladies" when it played the Shubert Theater in Los Angeles and has also played with greats such as Lena Horne, Frank Sinatra, Diahann Carrol, Percy Faith, and Merv Griffin. Paul and his lovely wife, Joan, who is a principal with the Los Angeles City Schools, and their two children, Pier and Damien, make their home in the Los Angeles area. When asked to share his plans for the future Paul said, "My basic goal is just to continue playing good music whenever I can."

Recipe for Remembrance

"When I was young, my father used to say, 'If you want to be a professional musician, we're going to see to it that you take private lessons and that you'll be able to read music and handle yourself in any situation.' At the time I didn't understand but as I grew older I was very grateful to my father for doing that."

Recipes

When we asked Paul if he cooks, without hesitation he said, "Sure. In my family, as far back as I can remember on both my mother's and father's sides of the family, everyone knew how to cook." With Joan's demanding schedule, his culinary talents have come in handy in the Humphrey household.

Since Paul suffers from an ongoing case of "sweet tooth," he shared two of his favorite

cake recipes. Sin Cake, which Paul says barely hits the table and vanishes, evolved through Joan's family, and Margaret Humphrey's Pound Cake is from his mother.

SIN CAKE

1 cup sifted flour
1½ cups chopped nuts
1 stick melted butter
1 (8 ounce) package cream cheese
1 cup powdered sugar
2 (8 ounce) cartons non-dairy whipped topping
2 (3½ ounce) packages instant pudding mix, any flavor
3 cups milk
1 tsp. vanilla extract

First layer
Mix the flour, 1 cup nuts, and melted butter in the bottom of a 13" x 9" x 2" baking dish. Pat firmly into the dish then bake at 350 degrees for 15 minutes. Cool.

Second layer
Mix well the cream cheese and powdered sugar then fold in one (8 ounce) carton of non-dairy whipped topping. Spread over the cooled, baked crust. Place in the refrigerator.

Third layer
Mix the instant pudding, milk and vanilla

together then pour over the cream cheese layer.

Fourth layer

Top with the remaining carton of non-dairy whipped topping and sprinkle with ½ cup finely chopped nuts, if desired. Keep refrigerated.

MARGARET HUMPHREY'S POUND CAKE

1 pound pure creamery butter
2¾ cups sugar
8 large eggs
4 cups sifted, white flour
4 Tbsp. coffee cream
2 tsp. vanilla extract

Cream the sugar and butter well then beat in the eggs, one at a time, until the mixture is very fluffy. Alternately add the flour and cream to the creamed mixture. Add the vanilla. Pour into a greased and floured angel food cake pan and bake 2 hours at 250 degrees then another 1½ hours at 275 degrees. Test doneness with a toothpick. The cake may also be baked in two 9" x 4" x 3" loaf pans at 350 degrees for 1¼ hours, until golden brown. Frost with Donut Shop Lemon Icing.

DONUT SHOP LEMON ICING

Combine 2 cups of powdered sugar with enough fresh lemon juice to make the icing smooth (approximately 2 to 3 Tbsp.). Spread on the cake or make the icing thinner and drizzle it on individual slices.

Pier

Damien

Jack Imel

Fast-stepping, marimba-playing Jack Imel was a performer with the Lawrence Welk Show for twenty-five years. Born and raised in Portland, Indiana, he graduated from the Arthur Jordan Conservatory of Music in Indianapolis, where he was spotted by bandleader Horace Heidt. He toured with Heidt's "Opportunities" show for eighteen months, then enlisted in the Navy in 1952. He was assigned to the Admiral's Band of the

Pacific Fleet during his Navy career and in 1955 won first place in the All-Navy Talent Contest. The prize was an appearance on the Ed Sullivan Show.

He joined the Musical Family after his discharge in 1957. He was promoted to producer and eventually to production manager, thanks to the innovative way he staged production numbers. Jack told us, "I would study the lyrics of a song and if it had a cute story line, I'd incorporate that into a skit. And, I believed the show should use a lot of people in the numbers so I came up with skits that involved the whole cast."

Jack is still actively performing. You might catch him at your county fair or on a cruise ship in the Caribbean. He and his wife Norma have been married since 1952 and live in the Los Angeles area. They boast five children and five grandchildren.

Recipe for Remembrance

"Two weeks before I got out of the Navy, I was contacted by the Welk office to audition at the Aragon Ballroom. Lawrence didn't have a marimba in the band at that time so he asked me to play on the show that next Monday night. There I was, in my Navy uniform, the Korean war going on at that time, and Lawrence hired me right on the spot. That had such an impact that people still come up to me and say they remember that night. It was the most memorable moment in my twenty-five years on the show."

Recipe

Jack confided that he is strictly a steak and potatoes man. He dug his favorite midwestern dessert from the family recipe files. "I'd eat one of these every day when I was a kid. Every restaurant in town had sugar cream pie." We agree, it's good enough to eat everyday.

SUGAR CREAM PIE

5 level Tbsp. flour
1 cup granulated sugar
½ cup firmly packed brown sugar
1 (13 ounce) can evaporated milk
4 Tbsp. butter
cinnamon

Mix the flour and sugars well, blend in the milk and butter then pour into an unbaked pie shell. Sprinkle with cinnamon and bake at 350 degrees for 45 to 60 minutes, until it rises to a round mound in the center.

Mary Lou and Jack

Lois and Lawrence

Lois Lamont Klein

When Lois Lamont and her date went to see Lawrence Welk perform one evening in Milwaukee, Wisconsin, in 1945, she had no idea she'd end up employed as his executive secretary for thirty-seven years. She and her escort happened to run into Mr. Welk before the show and he invited them to watch from back stage. Later, they went out with him for a bite to eat and he mentioned that he was in need of a secretary. In those days, it meant going on the road and touring with the band. It took a lot of convincing but Lois finally got her parents' permission after they met with Lawrence's attorney and some of the staff members.

In 1955, when the show went national, Lois was so flooded with work she asked her sister, Laurie, to come out from Wisconsin and be her assistant. She stayed all these years and officially took over Lois' job when she retired in 1982. Lois met Russ Klein when he joined the show in 1957. They were married in 1975.

Recipe for Remembrance

"Being Mr. Welk's secretary certainly hasn't been dull. When I first took the position I had no idea what my new job would entail. One of my first duties was to count the audience as they arrived, since the bands in those days were paid on a commission according to how many people attended. I remember once, when the doors opened at a midwestern ballroom, some huge farmers charged in and almost knocked me down!"

Recipe

She was always too busy with her career to devote much time to domesticity. Lois joked, "This recipe for Cherry Gelatin Salad is the extent of my cooking ability."

CHERRY GELATIN SALAD

2 (3 ounce) packages orange gelatin
¼ cup pecans, diced
1 (16 ounce) can black Bing cherries
12–15 pimento-stuffed green olives, halved
½ pint sour cream
2 Tbsp. sugar
1 tsp. vanilla

Dissolve gelatin in 2 cups very hot water. Add ½ cup cold water. Drain the cherries and add the juice. Stir in the cherries, pecans, and olives. Pour into a medium-sized glass baking dish and refrigerate until partially set (approximately 1 to 1½ hours). Stir and refrigerate until firm. Cut into squares. Add sugar and vanilla to the sour cream and spread over the salad before serving.

Russ Klein

Russ Klein, whose melodic saxophone enhanced the Lawrence
Welk Orchestra for twenty-five years, is a native of Mas-
sachusetts. He played with the Freddy Martin Orchestra from 1936 to 1949,
except for a time out to serve as a crew member of a B-24 in the Army Air
Corps. He played at the famous Coconut Grove nightclub in the Ambassador
Hotel in Los Angeles for years, did free-lance work for all of the major motion

83

picture studios, and performed on various television programs.

Russ had worked with George Cates, who later became music director for the Welk organization, at Coral Records. One evening in 1956, when the orchestra needed a substitute for an ailing saxophone and clarinet player, he phoned Russ and asked him to fill in. In July of 1957, he was called as a permanent member of the Musical Family and stayed until 1982, when he and his wife, Lois, retired. Although they miss the hustle and bustle of doing the show, the Kleins are enjoying taking it easy and traveling to places like Hawaii and New Zealand.

Recipe for Remembrance

"I miss playing with the Lawrence Welk Orchestra very much. They were all such fine musicians and I miss the companionship we all had. I'll never know a nicer bunch of people."

Recipe

Russ claims he's the chef in the Klein household. His wife, Lois, who was Lawrence's executive secretary, spent so much time on the road she never learned to cook. "She's a superb fisherwoman, however. She has a house in Wisconsin on the Mississippi River and can fish eighteen hours a day...while I play golf." Russ says his Pepper Steak is quite common, but is simple and tasty, and definitely a favorite of his.

Russ and Lois

PEPPER STEAK

1 lb. boneless round steak
1 Tbsp. soy sauce
1 clove garlic, minced
¼ cup salad oil
1 green pepper, cut into 1" squares
1 large onion, cut into 1" squares
½ cup celery, coarsely chopped
1 tsp. cornstarch
¼ cup water
2 tomatoes, cut into eighths
1 can pineapple chunks, drained

Cut steak into 1" cubes. Marinate in soy sauce, garlic, and salad oil for 2 hours. Fry in very hot skillet or wok until brown. Add pepper, onion, and celery and stir-fry for 5 minutes, until vegetables are crunchy but tender. Mix cornstarch with water and add to meat. Mix well. Add tomatoes and simmer 5 minutes. Add pineapple and heat. Serve over rice. Serves 4.

The Lennon Sisters

Several years have passed since the four charming girls from Venice, California captured the hearts of America. Still today, when people think of Lawrence Welk and the Musical Family, they think of the Lennon Sisters. To their fans, Dianne, Peggy, Kathy, and Janet, who literally grew up on the show, were the girls next door.

Janet reminisced about how they were "adopted" into the Musical Family. "We used to listen to our uncles singing harmony and began to pick it up by ear. We started singing for church functions. In 1954, when we were singing for such an occasion, our father's boss heard us and enjoyed our music, so he asked us to perform for a luncheon at the Lion's Club to which he belonged. We were paid $10.00. We were so thrilled! After that, we started performing for other groups."

"Dee Dee and Larry Welk, Jr., attended the same high school. He invited her to a Halloween party in 1955 and she said she couldn't go because she had to sing that evening. He offered to come and hear us sing then take her to the party afterward. He was impressed with our performance. He told Dee Dee that his Dad had a new television show and suggested that we sing for him some time. Larry followed through and called us for an audition at the Welk home. Mr. Welk liked us enough to call George Cates and set up a formal audition. Our first official performance was on the Christmas show in 1955."

The Lennons are a close-knit, Catholic family who incorporate their Christian faith into every aspect of their lives. Peggy reflected on some of the values their father instilled in all of his children. "First of all, my Dad had a sense of humor that bordered on the ridiculous. Our whole family is that way. On his serious side, he had it all together as far as life is concerned. He told us if we wanted to go out and sing, and if he and Mom didn't feel it was detrimental to us in any way, then we could. But, he said, 'The minute you feel you don't want to do it, we'll stop.'"

"He also told us that the only reason we were accepted by the public was because we had talent and reminded us that we couldn't make a living unless that audience was there. He taught us to respect that every person in the organization had a job and that our job wasn't any more important than theirs. He made us realize we couldn't sing if the technicians weren't doing their jobs or if the band members weren't playing their instruments. He taught us professionalism. He said if we were going to do something, we should do the best we could. That applied to homework as well as performing. He expected us to be prepared and to be one step ahead all of the time."

"Dad also told us that every person whose life we touch will be either better or worse for having met us and that we'd better decide which it was going to be. He loved people and he believed that making someone feel welcome and wanted was more important than indulging ourselves."

When we asked Kathy if she felt starring on a national television show during those formative years had affected their egos and attitudes, she replied, "We're still considered the Lennon kids who lived around the corner and happened to sing on the Lawrence Welk Show. We've always looked at it as just a job. It wasn't our whole life. We didn't strive to get this. We didn't go out on lots of interviews and auditions. It just fell into our laps."

"We had the closest thing to a normal upbringing that we could possibly have. Mom and Dad always said they didn't want us going to a Hollywood professional school or being taken away from our friends that we had since we were little. So we went to St. Marks Grammar School and St. Monicas High School. We went to football games and such. In fact, each of us was a homecoming queen or princess."

"Still, we were on the road a lot, but when we were gone we'd get our assignments from the nuns and do our homework and when we got back it was back to the routine. We all got good grades, although Peggy and Janet didn't have to work as hard to get theirs. They're naturally brighter. Dee Dee and I had to work hard for our A's."

When they married and had children, the four of them decided they wanted to spend more time with their families, so they did less touring and television. Presently, they only do four or five appearances in the spring and summer. They accept only benefits or Christian programs during the school year or holiday season. Despite their low profile, these vivacious women are still extremely popular. Kathy noted, "We're very, very surprised all the time when people still stop us on the street and say, 'Oh, my golly, I watched you forever! I played with your paper dolls.' The popularity is still there and we have been very fortunate and very blessed to be able to do the things we wanted to do."

But the Lennon Sisters are not just a group. They are four totally different individuals who are bonded by a great love. We thank them for sharing personal glimpses of themselves with us. Their biography, tentatively titled SAME SONGS—SEPARATE VOICES, will be released in 1985 by Round-table Publishing.

♪Dianne "DeeDee" Lennon Gass♪

Dee Dee, the oldest Lennon Sister, had just turned sixteen when the group joined the Musical Family. "We weren't too grown up," she reminisced. "We were still little girls."

She played "mother hen" to her three younger sisters when they were on the road. "Our Dad went with us and Mom stayed home with all of our little brothers and sisters. I had a big responsibility but I loved it. I enjoyed taking care of Janet, combing her hair and things like that."

Since leaving the Lawrence Welk organization, Dianne has devoted herself to her other two professions, homemaking and teaching. "I teach reading in kindergarten. Before that, I taught first grade reading to bilingual students. We have quite a Mexican population in the school and a large percentage of those children do not speak English at home, and are not spoken to in English either. So reading is difficult because they have trouble knowing what things are called in English."

In 1960 Dianne married the boy next door: well, actually, he was the boy across the street. "Dick's family moved here from Buffalo, New York, when he was nine years old and they lived across the street from Grandmother Lennon. They had a large family too; eight children. Dick's younger brother and I went to school together. Each of his brothers and sisters went to school with one of my brothers and sisters so our families were very good friends. Dick was in high school when I was in grammar school so I didn't really know him, but when I graduated from high school he called me and asked me out. That was it." Dick has been employed by General Telephone Company for twenty-six years and is presently a community relations manager in the Marina Del Rey office.

The Gass' have three grown children. Mary is studying nursing and Dee Dee wants to sing. She is studying under vocal coach Gene Merlino and wants to do commercials and background singing. Tommy is also musically inclined and has a band with his cousins. "It's strange to me," Dianne mused, "that two of my three children would want to do something in the music business because of all four of us sisters, I'm probably the one who likes performing the least."

Dianne's future goals are to see her children happy in what they're doing and to continue teaching. "We do most of our performing in the summertime because of schedules and jobs and kids in school. I'd like to teach full time once we're not singing. I really enjoy small children. I could be around them all the time."

Recipe for Remembrance

"I don't know what the other girls said, but we've had some funny things happen. In the early days we didn't have electric hair rollers or blow dryers. When we went on one nighters with the band, we performed every night and flew all day to get to our next destination. I mean, we traveled with curlers in our hair or with wet heads. It was very difficult. Also, we had to wash and iron our own clothes. Laundromats were just becoming popular then, but we didn't have time in every town to wash our clothes. We'd fly into a city, check into the hotel, eat dinner if we had time, then take our clothes to the arena where we were performing and iron them and get our hair set."

Recipes

The recipes Dee Dee contributed are personal favorites. "The Sherry Wine Cake is from a friend. She and her husband are like another set of grandparents to our children. They used to come over every Monday night and watch Little House on the Prairie with us. We'd take turns making dessert and when she made this cake, I loved it. Now it's what I make as gifts at Christmas time because it smells so good with the nutmeg and cinnamon. It's really a nice gift and very special to me."

"Dick and I used to take the kids to the beach every Saturday. We'd get up early in the morning and be gone all day. I'd put the Spanish Roast Brisket in the oven and let it cook all day. It didn't matter what time we got home. Dinner was ready." Dianne cautioned to make sure that the brisket is tightly wrapped so the juice doesn't seep out, or the meat will be too dry.

SHERRY WINE CAKE

1 package yellow cake mix
1 (3¾ ounce) package instant vanilla
   pudding
¾ cup salad oil
¾ cup sherry wine
4 eggs, unbeaten
½ tsp. nutmeg
1 tsp. cinnamon

Mix all of the ingredients then beat on medium speed for 5 minutes. Pour into a well-greased bundt pan and bake at 350 degrees for 45 minutes. Cool 15 minutes before removing.

ITALIAN DRESSING

¾ cup oil
¼ cup vinegar
2 Tbsp. sugar
⅛ tsp. salt
⅛ tsp. pepper
⅛ tsp. garlic salt
½ tsp. paprika

Combine ingredients. Shake and pour!

SPANISH ROAST BRISKET

Sprinkle 1 envelope of dry onion soup mix and ½ cup Mexican chile salsa over a 3–5 lb. beef brisket. Wrap tightly in heavy-duty aluminum foil. Place in a baking dish and bake all day (8–10 hours) at 275 degrees.

l. to r. Mary, Diane, Dick, Dianne and Tom

♫ Peggy Lennon Cathcart

Peggy was only fourteen years old when she joined the Musical Family. She thoroughly enjoys her career, but in a very different way than many fans might imagine. She told us, "There's something very special about being on stage. Not the fact that it's wonderful to be a performer, but I look across and I see Kathy and Janet as we come on different sides of the stage. They're so pretty and alive and the sound that we make together is beautiful. It's very fulfilling; rewarding. It just makes me feel good. These are my sisters and we're really good friends. The applause isn't necessary. It's the togetherness that is important. But we could sit in the living room and sing like that too, and get every bit as much enjoyment as doing it on stage."

Peggy shared how being a young television star affected her personally. "We never really had a choice in the kind of work we were going to do. Most kids talk a lot about what they're going to be when they grow up. I was never able to do that. I still say, when I quit singing I'm going to be a... I always wanted to be a teacher but never had the opportunity to go to college because we were always working. Not that I resented or hated the work, but the freedom to choose wasn't there. I would have liked to have been an archeologist. I think we missed making those kind of choices in our lives yet I think we were basically very satisfied with what we were doing."

Athough she'll always be a Lennon Sister, Peggy is also pursuing several other careers: she is a wife, mother, grandmother, and teacher. "I'm teaching at a Catholic boy's high school. I'm the only junior class religion teacher. I teach history of the Old Testament and Social Justice. And, I have a little drama club at the grammar school across the street. We build sets and make costumes and put on programs for the parish."

Peggy and her husband, Dick Cathcart, who is also a former member of the Musical Family, have nine children (three from Dick's previous marriage) and three grandchildren. Peggy shared that her philosophy of parenting centers on unconditional love. "Nobody has to live up to anything. You just love. Unconditional love is very freeing. It keeps you from being hurt."

Although she's been married over twenty years, Peggy sounds like a newlywed when she talks about her husband. "Dick is a studio musician. He plays trumpet and does a lot of jazz. He's a marvelous musician and a marvelous husband. At the time we got married, a lot of people gave us a very short time. But I can honestly say that nobody has the kind of marriage that I have. Dick is the finest man in the whole world. He's a giver and supports me in everything I do."

As for the future, Peggy wants to keep on doing what she's doing and explore whatever possibilities the Lord puts in her path.

Recipe for Remembrance

"We enjoyed the relationships we had on the show with the behind the scenes people; the engineering crew and electricians, the people at the studio. We also loved the musicians. The experience of doing live television was unique. We learned discipline and professionalism at a very early age."

Recipes

With nine children, we assumed Peggy would have to know how to cook. "My kids love fast foods, and so do I. I like crockpot cooking, particularly when I'm working steadily. I like the old family recipes, too. Our mother's mother is Mexican so all of those recipes are family favorites; the enchiladas, beans and rice. I'm the kind of cook that just throws things together. I go by looks and taste."

Peggy "threw together" two Cathcart recipes that are quick and easy to prepare, as well as nutritious and economical. We're sure every busy reader will relish her contributions.

ZUCCHINI CASSEROLE

6 medium zucchini
1 lb. lean ground beef
7 cups tomato sauce
2 cups ricotta cheese
2 cups mozzarella cheese, grated
1 cup parmesan cheese, grated
2 cups cheddar cheese, grated
¼ cup sugar
1 Tbsp. parsley flakes
1 egg

Slice the zucchini thin and parboil or steam just until tender. Drain and set aside. Brown and drain the beef. Add 6 cups tomato sauce. In a separate bowl, combine the ricotta, mozzarella, and parmesan cheeses, sugar, parsley flakes and egg. Pour 1 cup tomato sauce in the bottom of a 9"x 13"x 2" pyrex baking dish. Layer the zucchini, cheeses, and the meat mixture, ending with the meat mixture on top. Sprinkle with cheddar cheese and bake at 350 degrees for 45 minutes, until bubbly. Serves 8.

KIDS WHO HATE BREAKFAST DRINK

1 envelope vanilla instant breakfast
3 Tbsp. undiluted, frozen, orange juice
  concentrate
1 egg
1½ cups milk
1 large scoop vanilla ice cream.

Mix in blender and enjoy!

Peggy's husband, Dick   Peggy, with l. to r. Juli, Chris, Mike, Jennie, Betsy and Joe

Kathy Lennon Daris

Kathy was twelve years old when she started performing on the Lawrence Welk Show. She reflected on how the Musical Family was like a second family to her. "The beginning was marvelous. ABC was so small. We were the only studio. At that point Studio E was one building. There was one little room for the news and that was it. They had Chuckles the Clown and later, Soupy Sales, and we'd run over and watch them, then come back and do our show. We parked in the dirt lot and would string a volleyball net between two big lightposts and play during lunch while we ate our sack lunches."

"Between the electricians and stage hands and engineers and prop guys we were really like a family. And all us girls on the show took time to be a family. There were the four of us, Alice Lon, who was the Champagne Lady, then later, Norma and Jo Ann Castle. Barbara danced with Bobby. We all dressed in one great big room and we'd have pot luck. We had our special days, and baby and wedding showers. We were really close."

Kathy is a relative newlywed. She married Dr. Jim Daris, a chiropractor who specializes in sports and dance injuries, in April of 1982. "We met through my mom and three of my brothers and two of my sisters who were going to him as their doctor. I was having some problems with dizzy spells and pain in my back so my family said, 'Why don't you go to Dr. Daris? He's done so well with all of us.' Everytime they got a cold or stubbed a toe all I heard was Dr. Daris will take care of it. So when they said that to me, I said, 'Okay, but if he doesn't fix me then I don't want to hear his name mentioned again in this house.' I mean, everything was Dr. Daris this, Dr. Daris that. It was really funny."

"After he started treating me, my dizzy spells went away so I continued to see him on a maintenance treatment program. Not only was he a wonderful doctor, but we started dating and were married two and one half years later. Now he's my wonderful husband."

Kathy said she thinks a lot about her personal future goals. "Eventually, I hope to work with my husband. People always laugh at me when I say this, but I always wanted to be a secretary. I'm very logical and methodical and I love to do paper work, and filing and typing. I've had a lot of secretaries say to me, 'Do you know how I'd love to be up on the stage singing?' I guess the grass always looks greener, but I have always wanted to be a secretary."

Kathy shared another ambition. "In God's timing, I want to sing Christian music. Ministering through singing means a great deal to me. Also, I want to enjoy each day for what it is. I have two eyes, a nose and a mouth. I can hear and see and smell and taste and sing. I have two hands and two feet. I just want to enjoy the Lord's blessings."

Recipe for Remembrance

"We have many people come to us or write and say that they sort of adopted us as their family because they didn't have one. The other day a girl told me that she had been an abused child. She had no family of her own and was raised in a foster home, so she thought of our dad as her dad, and our mom as her mom, and us girls as her sisters. She told me how much happiness we've brought into her life and how our faith in God really made her hold on and believe that everything would turn out all right. It has been very special to feel that in some way I have touched millions of people with love."

Recipes

Kathy gave us a Lennon family staple that reflects her Mexican heritage. She suggests that you serve the Chiles Rellenos with flour tortillas that have been buttered, warmed, and rolled. A tossed green salad, and Hot Fruit Compote for dessert, rounds out this delicious, nutritious meal.

CHILES RELLENOS

1 (7 ounce) can whole Ortega green chiles
½ lb. Monterey Jack cheese, grated
½ lb. cheddar cheese, grated
1 cup biscuit mix
3 eggs
3 cups milk

Kathy and Jim

Split the chiles then rinse and remove seeds. Dry on a paper towel then arrange on the bottom of an 8"x11"x1½" baking dish. Sprinkle the grated cheeses evenly over the top of the chiles. Beat the eggs then add the milk and biscuit mix and blend well. Pour batter over the cheese and chile layer. Sprinkle with seasoned salt and bake in a preheated oven at 325 degrees for 50–55 minutes, until golden brown. Serve hot. Top with salsa for extra zing. For extra protein, add shredded, cooked chicken after the chile layer. Serves 8.

HOT FRUIT COMPOTE

2 packages macaroon cookies
1 (28 ounce) can peach halves
1 (28 ounce) pear halves
1 (28 ounce) can apricot halves
1 (28 ounce) can pitted plums
1 (28 ounce) can pineapple tidbits
½ cup (1 cube) butter
4 Tbsp. sherry wine

Crumble the cookies into a bowl. Drain the fruit, saving the pineapple liquid. Butter a 3 quart casserole then layer the crumbs and fruit alternately, ending with the crumbs. Dot each layer with butter. Drizzle the sherry and 4 Tbsp. pineapple juice over the top. Bake in a preheated oven at 350 degrees for 1 hour. Serves 6.

♪ Janet Lennon Bahler

J anet, the youngest Lennon Sister, was only nine years old when
she debuted on the Lawrence Welk Show. That was the same
year her grandfather died and Lawrence became a surrogate grandpa to
her. "He played games with us girls and was very warm and loving. There

weren't many people on the show and there was a lot of time for personal togetherness."

Since leaving the show, although she does personal appearances with her sisters, Janet has devoted most of her energy to being a wife and mother. Her husband John, writes, sings, records, and produces radio and television commercials. They have five children and three Arabian horses, which her daughters and husband ride in competition. She is very family oriented. "I have a wonderful family. My children are just the best. I'm enjoying raising them and I really haven't focused my sights much past getting them raised."

When asked about her plans for the future, Janet mused, "I don't know. I really don't have any strong feelings as to what I want to do with my life. I've never had a choice as to what to do. I've always been directed and sort of followed whatever anybody told me to do. Now, I'm thinking, oh! I'm going to have a chance one of these days to do what I want. I've been interested in creative writing. Possibly, I will go to college. Maybe help John in his business. I do know I want to keep busy."

Recipe for Remembrance

Janet shared what it's like to belong to such a large family. "When we get together for the holidays there are about 150 of us. There are 60 cousins, 15 or so aunts and uncles, and each of us have at least 3 or 4 children. We bring pot luck and have a grand old time; even though sometimes we have people hanging from the rafters."

Although all of the Lennon children now have families of their own, they are still very close. Janet told us, "We still get a chance to socialize with each other. There are eleven of us and we were each born in a different month, so we get together once a month for a birthday celebration. Consequently, we see each other all of the time."

Recipes

Janet gave us two very special ethnic dishes. Arroz con Pollo reflects her own heritage. "My mother is Mexican-American and my grandmother is a full-blooded

Mexican, so my Mom makes fabulous Mexican food. We all have those recipes and cook a lot of different kinds of Mexican foods." Sweet and Sour Chicken Cashew is an oriental favorite in the Bahler household.

ARROZ CON POLLO
(Mexican Chicken and Rice)

4 whole chicken breasts
½ cup salad oil
½ onion, diced
1 cup rice, uncooked
1 (12 ounce) can tomato sauce
¼ lb. fresh mushrooms, sliced
2 cups frozen peas
2½ cups boiling water
garlic powder, to taste
salt and pepper, to taste

Skin and bone the chicken then cut into strips and fry in oil in a large skillet until browned. Remove from pan. Add uncooked rice to oil in pan and fry until golden brown. Add the onion, mushrooms, tomato sauce, water and seasonings. Stir well then add the chicken. Cover and simmer for 40 minutes. Add the peas during the last 10 minutes. Serves 4.

SWEET AND SOUR CHICKEN CASHEW

4 whole chicken breasts
½ cup flour
⅓ cup salad oil
1 tsp. salt
¼ tsp. pepper

Sauce
1 (13½ ounce) can pineapple chunks, in heavy syrup
1 cup sugar
2 Tbsp. cornstarch
1 large green pepper, very thinly sliced
¾ cup cider vinegar
1 Tbsp. soy sauce
¼ tsp. ginger powder
1 chicken bouillon cube
¾ cup cashews

Skin and bone the chicken then cut into strips. Coat with flour then brown in oil in a large skillet or wok. Place in a large baking dish and set aside. To make the sauce, drain the pineapple and reserve the juice. Add enough water to the pineapple syrup to make 1½ cups liquid. In a saucepan, combine the sugar, cornstarch, pineapple liquid, vinegar, soy, ginger and bouillon. Bring to a boil then cook for 2 minutes over medium heat, stirring constantly. Pour the sauce over the chicken and bake uncovered for 30 minutes in a 350 degree oven. Top with the pineapple, green pepper, and cashews and bake another 30 minutes. Serve over rice. Serves 4 to 6.

l. to r. John, Billy, Janet, John, Kristin, Greg and Michele

Barney Liddell

Trombonist Barney Liddell admits he gets a bit vain about being the senior member of the Musical Family. He was with the Lawrence Welk Orchestra for almost thirty-five years! Even though he is retirement age, Barney plans to continue working. "I'm still playing and I record and work with anybody who wants a band member. If I stop now I'll drop. I don't want to do that. I want to continue."

He and his wife, Marianne, a nurse who is Director of Maternal Child Care at the Tarzana Medical Center in the San Fernando Valley, met in Jacksonville, Florida, when he was on tour there. They were married in 1978.

Recipe for Remembrance

We know you'll be touched by Barney's honest, inspirational remembrance. We thank him for letting us include it.

"I've had to make some serious changes in my life. I used to be a drinking man; I was into heavy drinking. When I took a test and realized I was drinking too much I decided I had to do something about it so I got into a self-help group. There I discovered that God works through people. People who cared had pointed out to me how much I drank but I just ignored it. I must say in all honesty I was always critical of devout Christians like my good buddy Johnny Zell. Johnny tolerated me and loved me and after I asked his forgiveness he said he understood and that he knew what I was thinking in my heart."

Lawrence congratulating Barney

"With the Lord's help and good friends I've licked my drinking problem—a problem I never thought I had because my ego wouldn't let me admit it. When I faced the truth, I accepted the Lord into my life and went back to my Catholic faith. I know now I'm truly born-again, not because I hadn't known God but because I wasn't doing what He wanted for my life."

Recipe

The Liddell's gave us a luscious Refrigerator Dessert that Marianne got from her mother, Helen Flaherty, who lives in Buffalo, New York. It's so simple yet terribly showy; a perfect company dessert that can be prepared ahead.

REFRIGERATOR DESSERT

1 package yellow cake mix
1 (3 ounce) package *instant* vanilla
  pudding
1 cup milk
1 (16 ounce) can crushed pineapple with
  juice
1 cup whipped cream
Chopped nuts (optional)

Prepare the cake according to package directions. Cool. Mix the pudding, milk, and pineapple with juice and stir until thick. Pour over the cake. Top with whipped cream. Sprinkle with nuts, if desired. Cover and chill at least 5 hours.

Joe Livoti

Joe Livoti was first violinist in the Lawrence Welk Orchestra for over twenty years and stayed with the Musical Family until the show retired. When he was twelve he won a scholarship to study at the Boston Conservatory of Music. After graduating, he came to Hollywood where he secured a position as first violinist in the NBC staff orchestra. Its director was Gordon Jenkins. After five years he joined the Warner Brothers Studio staff orchestra and worked there for seventeen years before becoming a member of the Musical Family. Joe and his lovely wife, Erma, make their home in Studio City, California.

Recipes

What else would one expect from Joe Livoti but great recipes for Italian Spaghetti Sauce and Veal Scallopine?!

ITALIAN SPAGHETTI SAUCE

½ lb. ground round
1 lb. Italian sausage (hot or mild)
1 large onion, chopped
2 cloves minced garlic
1 (6 ounce) can tomato paste
1 (28 ounce) can crushed tomatoes
1 cup fresh, sliced mushrooms (optional)
½ tsp. salt
1 Tbsp. sweet basil leaves

Brown the sausage in a large kettle then drain off half of the fat. Add the ground round, onions and mushrooms and cook until brown. Add the tomatoes, tomato paste, basil and garlic. Simmer covered for 1½ hours. Serves 4–6.

VEAL SCALLOPINE

1½ lb. Veal Cutlet
¼ cup butter
1 cup mushrooms, finely diced
2 tsp. green onions, chopped
1 large clove garlic, minced
¼ tsp. rosemary
dash of salt
dash of pepper
½ cup beef stock
¼ cup sauterne wine

Cut veal into thin slices & pound very flat. Roll lightly in flour. Melt butter in skillet and brown veal slices evenly. Remove and place in baking dish. Combine mushrooms, green onions, garlic, rosemary, salt and pepper in skillet and sauté in butter. Add beef stock and wine and bring to a boil. Pour over browned veal in baking dish. Cover and bake in 350 degree oven for 30–45 min. Serves 4–6.

Richard Maloof

Richard Maloof's illustrious musical career spans three decades. After graduating from San Juan High School in Citrus Heights, California, he attended Sacramento State, U.C.L.A. and Los Angeles City College and worked part time as a musician. Richard explains,

"I started trying to make contact with people. I didn't know anybody and I don't know how it happened, but one day, after I'd been working some casuals in town, I got a call from Les Brown asking me to go to work for him."

He played as a regular member of that group until he was drafted. In 1967, after finishing his stint in the Army, he joined the Lawrence Welk Show where he played stand-up bass, as well as fenderbass, tuba, and guitar for almost sixteen years. During that time, Richard also did studio work, playing for television, films, commercials, and making records.

Now that the Lawrence Welk Show is in retirement, Richard is continuing his career as a studio musician and is taking private lessons to further hone his talent. He and his wife, Mary Lou Metzger, met while they were performers on the show and were married in 1973.

Recipe for Remembrance

"My most memorable time on the Welk show was when I first joined the group, the same year I got out of the Army. Going from the service right to the show was a nice thing. It was such a change. The Lennon Sisters were still on and it was just a beautiful experience."

Recipe

Richard readily admits that he leaves most of the cooking to Mary Lou. During his bachelor days he survived on simple dishes like steaks or hamburgers but he did have one specialty which he learned from a neighbor who was a soldier in the Israeli Army. "I would take a chicken and put the whole thing in a pot that was large enough to fit then boil it for 24 hours, on low of course, because I didn't want to burn down the house. I would dump everything I could think of into the water, including every kind of vegetable in my refrigerator. I would live on a batch of that soup for a week while I was going to school and working. It was very healthy."

Richard picked one of his favorite recipes, Sour Cream Sole, to share with us. He claims, "It's fantastic! It's easy to fix and cooks in just enough time to make a salad and a vegetable."

SOUR CREAM SOLE

8 sole fillets
1 tomato, sliced very thin
1 small onion, sliced very thin
1 green pepper, sliced very thin
1 cup sour cream
salt and pepper to taste
pinch of dill weed
1/3 cup water or white wine

Pour the water or wine, if preferred, into a 9" x 13" x 2" baking dish then arrange 4 fillets in the bottom of the dish. Sprinkle with salt and pepper. Cover with a layer of tomato, onion, and green pepper then spread with a thin layer of sour cream. Repeat the procedure. "Frost" the top with sour cream then dust with dill weed. Cover with foil and bake at 325 degrees for 1 hour. Serves 6–8.

Mickey McMahan

Mickey McMahan was the lead trumpet man in the Lawrence Welk Orchestra for seventeen years, but he's been making music for most of his life. His other credits include thirteen years with Les Brown, and positions with the Freddy Martin, Stan Kenton, Tex Beneke, and

Jerry Gray musical groups. He has worked as a trumpeter for all of the major motion picture studios and has appeared on numerous television shows, such as the Dean Martin Show, the Steve Allen Show, the F.B.I. Story, and the Bob Hope Show. He toured for fifteen years with Bob Hope's overseas Christmas shows and has been on three tours of Japan with Billy Vaughn. Mickey lives in Van Nuys, California, with his daughter, Jayme.

Recipe

The McMahan's shared a delectable variation on an old favorite.

CHEESE MEATLOAF

3 lbs. lean ground beef
1 small clove garlic, pressed
2 tsp. salt
1 beef bouillon cube
dash cinnamon
4 slices bread
1 cup milk
1 green pepper, chopped
1 small onion, chopped
¾ lb. cheddar cheese, cubed
2 eggs
pepper and Accent to taste
½ cup catsup

Combine garlic, salt, cinnamon, pepper, Accent, onion and green pepper in a large bowl. Trim crusts from the bread and soak in milk. Squeeze out and add bread to the mixture. Crumble in bouillon cube then beat in eggs. Add the beef and mix with hands until thoroughly blended. Pat one-third of the meat mixture into a 7"x 12"x 1½" baking dish. Arrange one-third of the cheese cubes over the meat mixture, approximately two inches apart. Repeat the procedure until cheese and meat are used. Top with catsup and bake 1 hour at 350 degrees. Serves 6–8.

Buddy Merrill

Buddy Merrill strummed his way into the Lawrence Welk Orchestra in 1955. After a stint in the military, where he was assigned to West Point Academy as an arranger and guitarist, he rejoined the Musical Family. He has produced eighteen albums for Accent Records since

1964. In 1974 Buddy left the show to pursue a music writing career. Since then he has penned a symphonic work, "Living Sea," as well as original compositions for tape programmers and television commercials such as RB Furniture. Buddy also co-produces and writes for some of Myron Floren's recordings.

Recipe

Buddy's pancake recipe gives a new zest to an all time breakfast favorite. His Crepes Ensenada make a delicious lunch or dinner and can be prepared in less than an hour.

RUTH'S PANCAKES

1 egg, beaten
1 cup dairy sour cream
1 cup buttermilk
1 cup sifted flour
1 tsp. soda
1 tsp. baking powder
1 Tbsp. sugar
½ tsp. salt

Combine the egg, sour cream, and butter-milk. Sift together the dry ingredients then add liquid mixture. Mix until the batter is moistened but lumpy. Do not overbeat! Spoon about ¼ cup batter onto hot griddle and cook until bubbles form on the top. Turn and brown the other side.

CREPES ENSENADA

Cheese Sauce:
¼ lb. butter or margarine (1 cube)
½ cup flour
1 quart milk
¾ lb. grated cheddar cheese
1 tsp. prepared mustard
1 tsp. MSG (optional)
dash pepper

Melt the butter and blend in the flour. Slowly add the milk and blend well. Stir in the grated cheese, mustard, salt, MSG and pepper. Cook over medium heat, stir-ring until smooth. Set aside while you prepare the crepes.

Crepes:
12 thin ham slices
12 flour tortillas
1 lb. Monterey Jack cheese, cut into ½ inch sticks
1 (4 ounce) can green ortega chiles, cut into ¼ inch strips

Place one slice of ham on each tortilla. Put one cheese stick in the center of the ham slice and top with a strip of chile. Roll the tortilla and secure it with a toothpick. Place the tortillas, slightly separated, in a greased 13" x 9" x 2" baking dish. Cover with cheese sauce. Sprinkle with paprika and bake at 350 degrees for 45 minutes. This recipe can also be prepared in the micro-wave. Cover the crepes with waxed paper and cook to 150 degrees or 10 to 12 minutes at full power. To brown, broil for 2 to 5 minutes in a conventional oven. Serves six.

Mary Lou Metzger

ince 1971, Mary Lou Metzger has enhanced the Lawrence Welk
Show with her effervescent personality and nimble feet. She was
born in Pittsburgh, Pennsylvania but moved to Philadelphia when she was
five years old. She was discovered when she was attending Temple University

in that city and had an opportunity to audition for the All American College Show. "I sang and was told that I would probably hear from the sponsors in about six weeks because they were booked that far in advance. Fortunately, someone cancelled so I was summoned to California within a week. When the publicity about a local girl going to California came out in Philadelphia, Bob Hawkinson, an assemblyman in my district who had gone to college with Myron Floren, called my parents and asked if I'd like to go to a taping. After the show I sang for Lawrence and he asked me to sing at the Palladium after I taped the college show. I did, and I was hired."

Since the show stopped production Mary Lou has continued working with Jack Imel, as well as on her own, along with doing television commercials and musicals. She says she loves acting and definitely wants to do more of it.

Recipe for Remembrance

"Probably the biggest highlight of being on the show is the friendships. The girls are like a sorority and even though we're no longer taping we see each other on a regular basis. There's still the contact, still the caring that will last a lifetime. And there's something about Lawrence. He is more than a personality. He's almost a historic figure. I was so aware of that when we did the final taping. There was a feeling of having been part of a sort of historic entertainment era."

Recipes

Unlike her husband Richard Maloof, Mary Lou loves to cook. Her recipes are family favorites that have come down through generations. "The Ham Chowder came from my Mom, Helen Metzger, and it's wonderful. The Cranberry Nut Bread originated with my Grandma, Louella Splann, who was also from Pennsylvania. She died about a month before I joined the show. It's a standard Christmas treat and the trick is to serve it hot."

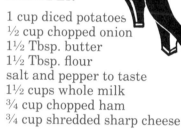

MOM'S HAM CHOWDER

1 cup diced potatoes
½ cup chopped onion
1½ Tbsp. butter
1½ Tbsp. flour
salt and pepper to taste
1½ cups whole milk
¾ cup chopped ham
¾ cup shredded sharp cheese

Boil the potatoes and onion until tender. Drain, saving one cup of the liquid. Blend together the flour, butter, salt and pepper then add the milk, potatoes and vegetable liquid. Cook and stir until the mixture thickens and bubbles. Add the ham and cheese and stir until the cheese melts. Serve topped with grated cheese. Serves 4.

CRANBERRY NUT BREAD

In a small mixing bowl combine 1 egg, 3 Tbsp. melted butter, and 1 cup sugar. Set aside. In a separate bowl mix:

2 cups flour
½ tsp. salt
Juice of 1 orange plus enough water to
    make ¾ cup
1 cup halved, fresh cranberries
1 cup coarsely chopped pecans
1½ tsp. baking soda
1 tsp. finely grated orange rind (optional)

Add the egg and sugar mixture to the fruit and flour mixture. Blend well. Pour into 2 greased and floured 6" x 3" loaf pans and bake at 325 degrees for one hour. Serve hot.

Tom Netherton

Tom Netherton is the handsome, bachelor singing star of the Lawrence Welk Show from 1973 to 1981. He hails from Bloomington, Minnesota, where his family settled after traveling for most of Tom's life, with his father, who was in the Army. Tom was "discovered" when some of

Lawrence's friends, Sheila and Harold Schafer, heard him sing in a little country church in North Dakota. They immediately told Lawrence about him.

"Lawrence and I met in Bismark. We talked and I sang for him, then he invited me to go to the St. Paul Civic Center a couple of months later, to sing as a guest on the show with the rest of the troupe when they were doing the show live."

Tom left the show in December of 1981 because he felt it was time for a change and a new challenge. Since then, he has done many secular and Christian concerts, and is concentrating on developing an acting career. "I'm finding that taking acting classes and performing have added a whole new dimension to my existence. When I did 'Oklahoma' I felt like a kid on stage for the first time. I was so excited. It was so much fun working with other people, instead of performing solo."

Recipe for Remembrance

During a telephone interview Tom laughingly related that "I travel so much that I get real tired of eating out in restaurants. When I have a few days at home I've been starting to do a bit more cooking and experimenting with the microwave. I've been so domestic I can't believe it. I'm even cleaning my own oven."

Recipes

Tom contributed a main dish and a dessert recipe that combine for one of his favorite meals. Both are "bachelor easy" to prepare. Strawberry Delight is from his mother, Lillian, and can be done ahead of time, since it has to refrigerate for at least three hours. Tom prefers it made with fresh, rather than frozen, berries.

STRAWBERRY DELIGHT

1 box yellow cake mix
3 pints sliced strawberries
1½ pints whipped cream, sugared to taste
½ cup granulated sugar

Prepare the cake mix according to package directions. Bake in a 9"x13"x2" pan. When the cake has cooled, cut it in half in the middle then slice the halves crosswise, making four pieces. Place a section of cake on a serving plate and cover it with sliced, sugared strawberries and a layer of whipped cream. Repeat with each cake section. Ice the entire cake with whipped cream and refrigerate for at least three hours, or overnight. This enables the strawberries and whipped cream to penetrate the entire cake. Garnish with 2 or 3 large, whole strawberries before serving.

PORK CHOPS CAROUSEL

4 pork chops, thick cut 1 to 1½ inches
1 large red Spanish onion, sliced
2 large ripe tomatoes, halved
1 green pepper, cut into rings
4 Tbsp. uncooked wild rice

Brown the pork chops on both sides then arrange in an oval baking dish. Top each chop with a slice of onion, 1 Tbsp. wild rice, a tomato half and a green pepper ring. Add ¼ cup of water then cover tightly and bake at 350 degrees for 2 hours. Serve with a tossed green salad and Strawberry Delight for dessert. Serves 4.

Elaine Niverson

Elaine Niverson, who is Bobby Burgess' third and present dancing partner, started dancing when she was five and confesses
she's always loved performing. "I used to put on acts on my front porch when I
was a little girl. I'd entertain the neighborhood and I loved it."

Elaine was born and raised in Dallas, Texas, then went to college at Sam Houston State University in Huntsville, Texas. After graduating, she did ballroom dancing then started teaching dance. That's when she met Bobby Burgess. "I was working in a studio in Houston and one of the fellows I worked with had corresponded with Bobby all of his life. One day, Bobby called Robin and said that he was looking for a new partner and would be auditioning for a replacement and wondered if he knew anyone. I flew out to the coast and auditioned with Bobby, really just for the fun of it, just to see what it was like. I didn't take it seriously at all. Then the next thing I knew, Bobby called me back and said that he had chosen me as one of three girls to come back and do a guest shot on the television show. I was chosen, and we started dancing together in March of 1979."

Since the show went off the air, Elaine and Bobby are still doing personal appearances around the country. She says she is "fiddling around" with the piano and taking acting lessons. This very busy lady lives in the Southern California area.

Recipe for Remembrance

Like many other members of the Musical Family, Elaine started her training early and never stopped her quest for excellence. "I've taken dancing lessons since I was five. In fact, mother started me in a dance class because (believe it or not) I was shy! She wanted to make sure that I got used to being with other children in a class type situation. I cried when I went for my first lesson. I was scared to death, but I loved it. I took lessons up through high school; tap, ballet, jazz, all kinds."

Recipes

All of Elaine's recipes are family hand-me-downs. She shared that she comes from a family of fabulous cooks but sees herself as an exception. "Believe me, I'm NO Betty Crocker!" Two of her contributions, Cheese Balls and Date Loaf, are from her mother, Dorothy Colvin, who lives in Dallas. The

soup recipe, which is so simple to prepare and delectably delicious, belonged to her grandmother, Willie Mae Smith.

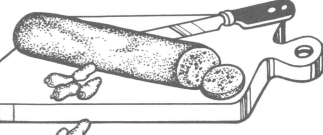

DATE LOAF

3 cups sugar
1½ cups milk
1 package finely chopped dates
1 tsp. vanilla
3 cups pecans, coarsely chopped

Mix the sugar and milk and cook to soft ball stage. Add the remaining ingredients and mix well. Shape into a roll as follows. Dampen a cotton or linen dish towel. Spread the towel onto a counter or table. Spoon the date mixture onto the towel and roll like a sausage until approximately 3 inches in diameter. (This recipe will make two long rolls.) When desired shape has been attained, roll the date loaf off of the dish towel onto a sheet of plastic wrap or aluminum foil. Wrap and seal tightly. This will keep in the refrigerator indefinitely. Cut into ¼" to ½" slices to serve.

ELAINE'S GRANDMOTHER'S SOUP

2 large potatoes, cubed
1 medium onion, chopped
1 (28 ounce) can tomatoes, cut into pieces
1 (6 ounce) can tomato paste
2 cups whole milk
1 tsp. baking soda
pinch red pepper

Cook the potatoes and onion in salted water until just tender. Add the tomatoes, including the juice, and tomato paste. Scald the milk with the soda then add to the tomato mixture. Simmer for about 10 minutes. Add the pepper. Serves 4.

CHEESE BALLS

2 cups grated cheddar cheese
½ cup softened margarine
1¼ cups flour
1 tsp. paprika

Blend the cheese with the margarine then stir in the flour and paprika. Mix well. Mold by teaspoonful into balls around green olives, ripe olives, cocktail onions, or pecans. Bake at 400 degrees for 10 to 15 minutes, until slightly brown. Serve hot. (These will freeze well and can be reheated in the microwave.)

Roger & David Otwell

The talents of Roger and David Otwell certainly brought double
the pleasure, double the fun, to Lawrence Welk fans for the five
years this duo appeared on the show. The identical twins were born in Tulia,
Texas and attended Lubbock Christian and West Texas State Colleges on a

full music scholarship. They credit their sister Barbara's father-in-law, Jack Love, with creating their show business break for them. The determined Mr. Love sent a demo tape to Ted Lennon, uncle of the famous Lennon Sisters and an executive with the Welk organization, and told him that Curt Ramsey, who screened new talent, already had a resumé and picture of the boys. At the same time, he wrote Curt Ramsey and informed him that Ted Lennon had a demo tape of them singing. The double entry speeded the hiring process.

At the time they came to the attention of Mr. Welk, Roger and David were doing shows for the governor of Texas and some state representatives, so many of them wrote letters on the twins' behalf. It wasn't long before Roger & David received a letter from Mr. Welk inviting them to do a guest shot. That quickly led to their being hired in 1977 and they stayed with the show until it went into retirement.

Roger and David both married girls from their hometown of Tulia, Texas. Roger and his wife, Millie, were high school sweethearts but didn't see each other for eight years after he left to go to college and establish a career. Millie continued her education and eventually studied opera in Austria. They started dating again when she came to Los Angeles and were married in December of 1981

On one of his many trips home David met his bride, Leslie O'Daniel, and after courting her long distance they were married in 1983.

This handsome duo now lives on the outskirts of Nashville, Tennessee. David shared that they live, "way up in the mountains," and that they do have neighbors but there's quite a distance between houses.

The Otwell twins have been busy in the last few years. They appeared for seven months at a club in the Smoky Mountains, during the World's Fair in Knoxville, Tennessee, and just completed thirty club dates throughout Texas. They've performed as the opening act for Louise Mandrell and have been doing a lot of songwriting, concentrating on gospel music. The boys shared that, "The Lord has really watched over us. You can't hurry events in your life. They just kind of happen when they're supposed to. We try to push it a lot, but I guess that's human."

Recipe for Remembrance

Roger's and David's fondest memory is the time Mr. Welk invited them to spend the night at his home. David related, "Mrs. Welk was really nice. She helped us get the guest room ready. She got up with us the next morning and we had breakfast together. She even taught us some card games. We got to know her well."

Roger recalled, "It was really a blast! We woke up to the sound of Mr. Welk doing laps in his indoor swimming pool at 5 A.M.! He's definitely an early riser. We were at the studio by 7:30. We got there so early we had to have a guard open up the dressing room for us." Both boys agree their visit to the Welks was a great experience.

Recipes

The twins modestly admitted that they were both fairly good cooks before they were married but that now they enjoy having their wives do the cooking for them. Their mother, Alyne, gave us a recipe for Roger's Favorite German Chocolate Cake, for David's favorite Corn Casserole, and for Otwell Christmas Salad, that has graced the family's holiday table for about fifty years. Alyne says it's superb with turkey and dressing.

ROGER'S FAVORITE
GERMAN CHOCOLATE CAKE

½ cup boiling water
1 package German sweet chocolate
1 cup shortening
2 cups sugar
4 eggs
1 cup buttermilk
1 tsp. baking soda
2½ cups flour
¾ tsp. salt

Melt chocolate in boiling water and set aside. Cream shortening and sugar until fluffy. Add eggs and cream well. Sift together the dry ingredients and add alternately with the buttermilk to the creamed mixture, beating after each addition. Add the chocolate and beat until smooth. Bake in three well-greased and floured 9" round pans at 350 degrees for 35 to 40 minutes.

ICING

3 eggs
1 cup sugar
1 (13) ounce can evaporated milk
1 tsp. vanilla extract
¼ cup (½ cube) margarine
1 cup flaked coconut
½ cup finely chopped pecans

Beat eggs then add the milk and sugar and cook in a double boiler until very thick. Add the remaining ingredients and beat until cool and thick enough to spread. Frost tops of layers only.

CORN CASSEROLE

1 bell pepper, chopped
2 ribs celery, chopped
2 Tbsp. margarine
1 (16 ounce) can whole kernel corn, drained
1 (16 ounce) can cream-style corn
1 cup cooked rice
½ tsp. salt
2 packets sugar substitute or 2 tsp. sugar
1 (4 ounce) jar pimentos, optional
1 cup cheddar cheese, grated

In a large skillet, sauté the pepper and celery in margarine. Add all remaining ingredients except the cheese and mix well. Pour into a casserole dish, top with cheese and bake uncovered for 25 to 30 minutes at 350 degrees, until cheese is brown and bubbly.

OTWELL CHRISTMAS SALAD

½ head iceberg lettuce, chopped
1 cup tender celery, chopped
1 large, unpeeled, red apple, chopped
1 large tomato, chopped
1 cup walnuts, coarsely chopped
2 Tbsp. mayonnaise

Combine all ingredients and toss with mayonnaise just before serving.

Back home in Tulia, Texas

Leslie and David

Roger and Millie

David and Roger

Charlie Parlato

Charlie Parlato, talented trumpet player and singer, and member of the Hotsy Totsy Boys Dixieland Combo, was a member of the Musical Family for twenty years. He moved to Los Angeles in 1942 and married his lovely wife Peg a year later. He freelanced and did radio and TV

121

shows with Red Skelton, Bing Crosby, Dennis Day, Harry James, David Rose, and Dinah Shore. He recorded and performed with greats like Horace Heidt, Kay Kayser, Mel Torme, Andy Williams and Tennessee Ernie Ford but admits, "I had a lot of hard times between shows."

Originally Charlie was hired as a regular on the Lawrence Welk Show just to play trumpet but when the producers heard that he sang and did comedy, they incorporated that into his routines.

Recipe for Remembrance

With Charlie's background, he could write a book about his experiences. He recalled for us a time in the mid-fifties when he was doing the Tennessee Ernie Ford television program. "The show ran five days a week. Until then, I'd always sung and played in the band. I started doing comedy routines with Ernie in the commercials. He loved to pick on me, in a sense of fun. That show lasted three years and it was one of the nicest, fun times of my career. I also greatly enjoyed playing with the Hotsy Totsy Boys. It was a lively group and got a lot of mail."

Recipes

Charlie is known as a fine cook within the Musical Family. Almost every performer has sampled his Cioppino (fish stew). The Mustard Dressing and Cottage Cheese Pancakes are his own concoctions and the Swedish Meatballs recipe was given to him by a longtime friend, Jean Valente.

Charlie gave us some interesting background information about the Cioppino. "This stew was popular with the Portuguese fishermen who fished off of the Southern coast of California in the 1800's. It is very rich, so I use unsalted tomato sauce. The fish is salty enough by itself. Also, you don't have to use the shell fish. It's quite fatty. A fisherman warned me lobster will get tough if you cook it too long so I always

add it last. I don't like to thicken the stew with flour, but you can do that if you want. I serve it with sourdough bread, a salad, and wine. It's wonderful!"

CIOPPINO
1 small onion, chopped
¼ lb. fresh mushrooms, sliced
2 carrots, sliced thin
1 clove garlic, crushed
½ cup green pepper, chopped
2 Tbsp. salad oil
1 (15 ounce) can unsalted tomato sauce
2 cups water
1 cup dry red wine
1 packet instant vegetable broth mix
½ tsp. Italian herb seasoning mix
⅛ tsp. seasoned pepper
1 lb. sea bass, cut into 1 inch pieces
12 small clams, washed in shell
6 ounces cleaned, deveined, shelled shrimp
1 small lobster tail, cut into strips
1 (8 ounce) package frozen Alaskan king crab
½ cup parsley flakes

Sauté the mushrooms, carrots, garlic, onion and green pepper in oil in a large dutch oven. Stir in the tomato sauce, water, wine, vegetable broth mix and seasonings. Cover and simmer 20 minutes, stirring occasionally. Add the bass, shrimp and crab. Cover and simmer 20 minutes. Add the lobster and clams and simmer another 20 minutes. Garnish with minced parsley flakes. Serves 6.

CHARLIE'S MUSTARD DRESSING

½ cup salad oil
2 Tbsp. cider vinegar
1 Tbsp. Dijon mustard
1 tsp. honey

Mix in blender for two minutes. Delicious on any salad.

SWEDISH MEATBALLS

Meatballs
¾ lb. lean ground beef
¾ cup fine bread crumbs
¼ cup minced onion
¾ tsp. cornstarch
pinch allspice
1 egg, slightly beaten
¾ cup milk
¾ tsp. salt
¼ cup salad oil

Combine the ingredients and shape into 30 to 32 small meatballs. Brown in oil on all sides in a large, heavy skillet. Remove and set aside.

Sauce
½ tsp. salt
3 Tbsp. flour
2 cups water
1 cup burgundy wine
2 beef bouillon cubes
⅛ tsp. pepper

Blend the flour with the remaining fat in the skillet. Stir in the water, burgundy, bouillon, and salt and pepper, then cook over medium heat, stirring until smooth. Arrange the meatballs in the sauce. Cover and simmer for 30 minutes. Serve over rice or fine noodles. Serves 4–6.

COTTAGE CHEESE PANCAKES

1 pint cottage cheese
4 eggs
3 Tbsp. whole wheat pastry flour
4 Tbsp. soybean oil or safflower oil
dash of salt

Blend cheese and eggs in blender until very smooth; add other ingredients, blend smooth. Bake on lightly greased griddle. Serve with applesauce, loganberries, blueberries or any frozen or fresh fruit, etc. "They are especially delicious when rolled into rolls with sour cream on the inside, reheated (to warm the sour cream) and served with melted butter and wild mountain blackberry syrup. But they are rather high in calories!"

Jimmy Roberts

Jimmy Roberts, popular tenor on the Lawrence Welk Show for twenty-seven years, was born in Kentucky. The "show business bug" bit him when he was in the Army after World War II and was asked to sing a song while the sets were being changed in an Army play. He went to

Hollywood after his discharge to study music at the Herbert Wall Music School.

Like several other performers, Jimmy found out he was hired when Lawrence announced on the air in 1955 that he was the newest member of the Musical Family. He originally auditioned to please his sister and brother-in-law. "I went down to the Aragon Ballroom and watched the cast rehearse. Lawrence walked by and said hello and asked if he could help me. I told him I was a singer who wanted to audition so he told me to take my music over to the pianist, Larry Hooper, and to sing. I sang 'Loveliest Night of the Year,' which I found out later Lawrence played on his accordian. I got a good reaction from the band and Mr. Welk, but he likes to get an audience reaction, so that very night I performed at the Aragon Ballroom. The audience liked me, too, but Lawrence didn't hire me for about three months."

While performing in Florida, Jimmy met a lovely widow named Vi Hammons. They were married in 1985 and presently live in Clearwater, Florida. As for the future, Jimmy said, "My goals are to live a happy life, to be around nice people, and to work as long as I can."

Recipe for Remembrance

"I'm pretty lucky, I think, to have worked in this business so long without too many disappointments. I did other jobs in between performing: at gas stations, building fences, and things lke that. I'm fortunate to have been with Mr. Welk as long as I was. I've met a lot of nice people and that's something to be thankful for."

Recipe

Jimmy confessed that he spends more time in the dining room than the kitchen. His recipe, straight from his bachelor kitchen, is the most "unique"??? of any in the collection. He suggests that if you don't want to spend time preparing it that you go out to your favorite restaurant instead. (He usually heads for Chasen's or Scandia when he can't face the stove.)

JIMMY ROBERTS' SANDWICH DELUXE

"Take two slices of white bread. It's best to scrape off the mold if there is any. Check the refrigerator for a suitable piece of cheese or retrieve some from the nearest mousetrap if there isn't any. Butter the bottom and sides of a frying pan. If no butter is available you can borrow from your neighbor. Put the cheese between the slices of bread. Brown both sides of the sandwich. You'll know it's done when it starts to smoke. Serve with garnish on a paper plate. Goes well with white wine, such as Ripple. I suggest you add Twinkies for dessert. They are a fitting touch to this meal. Bon appétit!"

Bob Smale

Bob Smale, former pianist, conductor and arranger for the Mary Kay Trio, joined the Lawrence Welk Band in 1969. Bob says his hiring was an accident, "a matter of being in the right place at the right time." He was filling in for the regular music director on a local network show at

NBC in Los Angeles when Bob Ballard, the musical supervisor of that show, recommended him to Lawrence. He auditioned and was hired. Because he's such a fine arranger, he was asked to arrange for many of the singers on the Lawrence Welk Show.

Bob met his lovely wife Mary in Las Vegas when she was a showgirl at the Sahara. She gave up her show business career when they were married in 1963. They have three children: Margaret, Rob and David, and make their home in the Southern California area.

Presently, Bob is free-lancing, mostly playing casual type engagements, and doing some writing. As for future plans, he says, "My number one goal is to try to get out of the music business."

Recipe for Remembrance

"I truly enjoyed meeting some of the people who had been writing to me, like a couple on the west coast of Florida. One seventy year old lady, who is quite talented, began writing to me and sending me little pieces of music. She was really something. I finally met her and her husband and developed a warm acquaintanceship with them. I still stay in touch with her and see her whenever I go to St. Petersburg."

Recipe

Since Mary received her black belt in Karate she is a very busy lady. She teaches a white belt class and is a substitute school teacher, so she and Bob split kitchen duty. Bob refers to himself as "an enthusiastic amateur." A native Southern Californian, Mary chose a unique recipe using one of the area's most prolific fruits, the pomegranate. "I've been making pomegranate juice and jelly ever since we moved into our house seventeen years ago and discovered a pomegranate bush on our property."

Indian Chicken, a dinner favorite at the Smale table, was given to them by a friend. Mary confesses, "I doctored it up and made
it into my own." Steak Sauce Diane is Bob's specialty that is widely admired by those who have sampled it.

POMEGRANATE JUICE
(for drinking or jelly)

Mary warns that pomegranate juice stains badly (at one time it was used as a dye), so suggests that you cover all surfaces in the work area, including sinks, appliances, and chairs, and that you wear light weight plastic gloves or plan to have purple hands for a few days.

Wash the pomegranates in a pinch of baking soda and warm water, then cut them in half. Juice them as you would an orange. (Mary says this job definitely calls for an electric juicer.) Strain the juice through a cheesecloth or stainless steel strainer, to remove seeds and pulp. Let the juice stand in the refrigerator for several hours, until any excess pulp settles to the bottom, then pour off the clear juice into appropriate containers.

POMEGRANATE JELLY

3½ cups pomegranate juice
¼ cup lemon juice
1 package MCP Pectin
1 cup light corn syrup
4½ cups granulated sugar

Mix the pomegranate and lemon juice in a 4 quart kettle. Sift in the pectin, stirring vigorously. Set the mixture aside for 30 minutes, stirring occasionally. Add the corn syrup and mix well. Gradually stir the sugar into the fruit juice mixture then warm over medium heat to 100 degrees. When the sugar is completely dissolved, pour it into clean jars and cover. Store in the freezer. When thawed, the jelly can be stored in the refrigerator for up to 3 weeks. Yields 48 ounces.

INDIAN CHICKEN

1 whole chicken, cut up, or the equivalent
   in pieces
2 cans cream of mushroom soup
¾ cup milk
3 Tbsp. curry powder
3 apples, peeled and diced
1 onion, finely diced
3 fresh tomatoes, diced
4 cups cooked rice

Lay chicken pieces flat in a shallow roasting pan. Cover loosely with foil and bake at 375 degrees for 1 hour. After the chicken is cooked, combine the soup, milk, and curry powder in a saucepan and simmer, stirring constantly until the mixture is thoroughly heated and well blended. Drain excess fat from the chicken then pour half of the soup mixture over the chicken. Save the remainder to use later as a sauce.

Cover the chicken with foil and place it in a 250 degree oven while preparing the rice, vegetables, and fruit. Cook the rice according to package directions. Dice the apples, onions, and tomatoes. Pour a little lemon juice over the apples to keep them from turning dark. Immediately before serving, reheat the curry-mushroom sauce. To serve, place a mound of rice on each plate and top with diced apple, onion, tomato. Add a piece of chicken and top with curry-mushroom sauce. Serves 4.

BOB'S STEAK SAUCE DIANE

1 onion flavored telma cube
1 vegetable flavored telma cube
2 shallots, diced
1 level tsp. dijon mustard
1 cup water
1 tsp. Worcestershire sauce
1 heaping Tbsp. sesame seeds
2 heaping Tbsp. commercial steak sauce
½ jigger brandy or 1 jigger dry red wine

Combine all of the ingredients. Crumble the telma cubes, which are available in the gourmet section of most supermarkets, into the mixture and simmer for 5 to 15 minutes. Delicious served on any kind of steak.

l. to r. Margaret, Rob, David, Mary and Bob

Don Staples

Don Staples, whose fine trombone playing added depth and originality to the Lawrence Welk Orchestra for seventeen years, joined the group immediately after he finished touring the United States with the San Francisco Ballet Orchestra and doing a series of concerts with the Roger Wagner Chorale. He also owned his own manufacturing business when he auditioned for, and won, a position with the Musical Family.

Don and his pretty wife, Betty, met while they were both students at U.C.L.A. and were married in 1963. They have two daughters. Sheryl won a full violin scholarship to Crossroads School in Santa Monica and Debbie is involved in drama and voice.

Since the show retired, Don has expanded his career by teaching trombone at U.C.L.A. and has stepped up activity in the Amway Corporation, where he is a Direct Distributor. He is also involved in producing and conducting Amway shows around the country.

Recipe for Remembrance

Don with daughters Debbie and Sheryl

Don reminisced about how humorous live performances can be. He related an incident that happened in Lake Tahoe during one of the group's annual appearances at Harrah's. "John Klein was the drummer at that time. He hated solos so wasn't too thrilled that he had to start a ten minute segment on the timpani, then quickly move to the drums. Apparently, during the transition, he missed the stool because suddenly we heard this huge crash of cymbals and turned to see drumsticks and feet flying. Then up came John with his eyes as big as saucers. Everyone in the band was laughing so hard we literally couldn't play anymore."

Recipes

Don gave us three fabulous recipes. The recipe for Company Strata comes from his mother, Donna Freeman, of Fullerton, California. Betty claims she gets most of her very best recipes from her talented mother-in-law. She says the strata can be prepared a day ahead if you prefer. She also alters the recipe to a side dish by omitting the ham. If she wants to serve it as a main dish, she includes the ham.

The Beef Jerky and Baked Stuffed Sweet Potatoes both are from Betty's sister, Grace Lusby, who now lives in Oakland, California.

COMPANY STRATA

12 slices white bread
12 ounces sharp, processed cheese, sliced
1 (10 ounce) package frozen, chopped broccoli
2 cups fully cooked ham, diced
6 eggs, slightly beaten
3 cups milk
2 Tbsp. instant minced onion
½ tsp. salt
¼ tsp. dry mustard

Cut 12 doughnuts and holes from the bread. Set aside. Arrange the crusts and scraps of bread in the bottom of a 13" x 9" x 2" baking dish. Layer the cheese, broccoli and ham over the bread. Arrange the doughnuts and holes on the top. Combine eggs, milk, onion, salt, and mustard and pour over the bread. Cover and refrigerate at least 6 hours or overnight. Bake uncovered at 325 degrees for 55 minutes. Let stand 10 minutes before cutting. Serves 12.

GRANDMA'S OVEN-DRIED BEEF JERKY

2½ lbs. lean boneless beef
1 cup water
2 Tbsp. liquid smoke
2 tsp. salt
1 tsp. garlic powder (optional)
1 tsp. onion powder (optional)
¼ tsp. black pepper

Select a lean cut of meat from which long strips can be sliced easily. Brisket flank steak, heel of round, or London broil are naturals and will be easier to work with if slightly frozen. Cut with the grain if you like chewy jerky or across the grain for a more tender morsel.

Trim all visible fat from the meat. Cut into strips that are 4" to 6" long, ½" to 1" wide, and ⅛" thick. Mix water, liquid smoke, salt, garlic and onion powders, and pepper. (For less highly seasoned jerky omit the garlic and onion powders.) Marinate overnight (at least 12 hours) in refrigerator. Drain and pat dry on paper towels. Cover the bottom rack of oven with aluminum foil. Hang or lay strips on top rack so they do not overlap. Dry meat at the lowest temperature setting (150 to 200 degrees) for 4 to 7 hours, until it browns, feels hard, and is dry. Let cool then remove from racks and store in an airtight container at room temperature. Keeps indefinitely.

BAKED STUFFED SWEET POTATOES

6 large sweet potatoes
¼ cup (½ cube) butter
¼ cup Amaretto liqueur
¼ cup heavy cream
¼ tsp. ground nutmeg

Scrub potatoes. Dry and bake in a pre-heated 425 degree over for 40 minutes or until done, or microcook according to manufacturer's directions. Cut potatoes in half, lengthwise, and scoop out the potato meat into a medium bowl, taking care not to break the shells. Set shells aside. Mash the pulp. Add butter, Amaretto, cream and nutmeg. Beat until light and fluffy. Carefully spoon back into the potato shells. Bake on a cookie sheet or in a large, glass baking dish in a 350 degree oven for 15 minutes. Serves 6.

l. to r. Don, Betty, Debbie and Sheryl

Kathie Sullivan

Kathie Sullivan, who hails from Kenosha, Wisconsin, always knew she would have a career in music, but the initial effort toward her dream began in junior high school when she started playing the bass! Her high school choir director urged her to study voice so she joined the school choir and studied music in college. She has been singing ever since.

She was discovered by Lawrence Welk in August of 1976 when she was selected from among fifty coed contestants to guest as the "Champagne Lady" for a Welk concert at the University of Wisconsin. The upshot of that appearance was an immediate invitation to join the Musical Family in Los Angeles.

Since the show went into retirement Kathie's interest has centered on gospel music, although she would like to include some musical comedy in her busy schedule. In 1982 she was named Female Gospel Singer of the Year and has just released a new album. She was thrilled to have been chosen by World Vision to share in their tour of the drought stricken areas of South Africa in 1984. She did this as a ministry, not to perform. Kathie shared, "I did sing but only because the people sang to us. It was a very humbling experience."

white on television so the wardrobe mistress dug out a peach-colored dress I hadn't worn in a long time. It had a big, wide belt that snapped in the front. I guess I had gained a little weight because the snaps kept popping open. This wasn't a problem when I was standing on stage but when I went out into the audience and sat on the man's lap and took a deep breath, all of the snaps popped open. They were taping so I made a joke about it and said, 'Oh, you're undressing me!' Everyone loved it."

Recipe for Remembrance

Kathie experienced many memorable, humorous moments as a member of the Musical Family. A mishap that could qualify as one of life's most embarrassing moments happened when she went out into the audience, sat on a man's lap and sang "Bill" from the musical "Showboat." This was part of a routine she often used when the group was on tour.

"Since this was our final tour, I was planning to wear a beautiful white, one-shouldered, chiffon dress but the producers didn't want me to wear

Recipes

Kathie contributed two recipes that have been handed down through her family. The Pumpkin Squares are from her grandmother, Leone Sullivan, and standardly replace pumpkin pie at Thanksgiving and Christmas in the Sullivan household. The Cashew Brittle is from Kathie's Mother, Betty Sullivan. Kathie says when she was a child they would put the cashew brittle on a cookie sheet and let it harden outside in the snow then she would have the fun of breaking it into pieces (the bigger the better) and nibbling in the process. The Chicken Drummettes À L'Orange is a personal favorite of Kathie's, and can be served as either an appetizer or a main dish.

PUMPKIN SQUARES

Crust:
1 cup flour
½ cup oatmeal
½ cup firmly packed brown sugar
½ cup softened butter

Cream the butter and sugar then add the flour. Mix well. Stir in the oatmeal and press into a 9" x 13" x 2" baking dish. Bake 15 minutes at 350 degrees. While the crust is baking, mix the filling.

Filling:
2 cups canned pumpkin
1 (13 ounce) can evaporated milk
2 eggs
¾ cup sugar
½ tsp. salt
1 tsp. cinnamon
½ tsp. nutmeg
¼ tsp. cloves

Combine all ingredients. Beat by hand until mixed well. Pour onto the crust and bake for 20 minutes at 350 degrees. While the filling is baking, mix the topping.

Topping:
½ cup chopped nuts
½ cup firmly packed brown sugar
2 Tbsp. butter

Sprinkle the topping over the filling and bake 20–30 minutes at 350 degrees, until the top springs back lightly.

CASHEW BRITTLE

2 cups sugar
1 cup light corn syrup
½ cup water
1 cup butter
2 cups roasted, unsalted cashews
1 tsp. baking soda

Heat the sugar, syrup, and water in a 3 quart saucepan, stirring until the sugar is dissolved. When the mixture boils, blend in the butter. Cook to 230 degrees, stirring often, then add the nuts. When the mixture reaches 280 degrees, stir constantly until it reaches 305 degrees then remove from heat and add the soda. Mix well. Pour onto a greased cookie sheet and spread evenly. "Cool in the refrigerator or on the back porch, if you live in Wisconsin. When it hardens, break into pieces or use for a doormat!"

CHICKEN DRUMMETTES À L'ORANGE

3 lbs. chicken wings
2 eggs, slightly beaten
½ cup frozen, undiluted, thawed, orange juice
1½ cup fine fresh bread crumbs
1½ cup ground pecans
1 tsp. salt
¼ tsp. pepper
¾ cup butter

Halve each wing and clip off the tip ends. (These can be set aside for later use, such as making broth.) In a shallow pan, combine the eggs and orange juice. In another, mix the bread crumbs, pecans, salt and pepper. Melt the butter and pour it into a 9" x 13" x 2" baking dish. Dip each piece of wing in the egg/juice mixture then roll it in the bread crumbs. Place in the buttered dish and bake covered at 350 degrees for 30 minutes. Turn and bake uncovered for 15–20 minutes, until golden brown.

Kenny Trimble

Kenny Trimble's musical career as a trombonist spans from the beginnings of the Big Band era into the contemporary eighties. He and his wife Bonnie met when her father was Kenny's scoutmaster. They married in 1942 when Kenny was a trombonist in an Army band in Texas.

135

After World War II Bonnie, Kenny, and their son Jimmy traveled with the Ray Anthony and Tex Beneke orchestras. Their daughter, Patti, was born in 1949. She and her husband live in Virginia City, Nevada, and have graced the Trimbles with three grandchildren. Jimmy and his wife Mary live in Las Vegas, where Jimmy plays first trombone at the Stardust Hotel.

Although Kenny claims he is now retired, he plays in the Virginia Municipal Band as well as performing in a small band at the Senior Citizens Club in Sparks, Nevada. Bonnie is busy doing oil painting. Landscapes, seascapes, and still life are her specialty.

Recipes

BLACK-EYED PEAS

2 cans black-eyed peas
1 green pepper, diced
4–6 slices of bacon, diced
1 onion, diced
salt and pepper to taste

Cut up the bacon and fry with the green pepper and onion until tender. Add the peas and stir occasionally until thoroughly heated.

K. T'S SPAGHETTI SAUCE

2 (32 ounce) cans spaghetti sauce
1 (4 ounce) can mushroom pieces, drained
1 lb. lean ground beef
3 mild Italian sausages
1 (1½ ounce) envelope spaghetti sauce mix
1 onion, diced
Italian seasoning mix, to taste

Empty the spaghetti sauce into a large pot. Add the drained mushroom pieces and spaghetti sauce mix. Sprinkle in Italian seasoning mix to taste. Brown the ground beef and diced onion in a skillet. Drain and add to the sauce mixture. Crumble and brown the sausage and add it to the sauce. Simmer 1 to 1½ hours, stirring frequently. Serves 6 to 8.

Jim Turner

Jim Turner, the good looking guitar strumming, bass-baritone country singer, was born and raised in Knoxville, Tennessee. His parents are both graduates of the Chicago Conservatory of Music. His mother majored in piano and his father in voice, so it was natural that he'd be a musician, too. He got his early experience performing in a local band on the southeastern college concert and club circuit. He then toured Europe as a guest soloist and guitarist for the University of Tennessee choir.

Jim graduated from the University of Tennessee with a Bachelor of Science degree in Industrial Management. He felt he should have that to fall back on in case his music career didn't work out. After graduating, Jim moved to Nashville and launched a successful career in country music as a songwriter, session player, and recording artist.

While on a trip to New York, Jim auditioned for "Jesus Christ Superstar" and landed the role of Pilate in the original cast. After the Los Angeles run of the play, he decided to stay on the west coast but to return to his country music roots. It wasn't long before his career was blooming and he was signed to recording and publishing contracts.

Russ Klein, a saxophonist with the Lawrence Welk Orchestra, discovered Jim when he was performing at a private party. He told Jim he thought Mr. Welk would like his work and asked if he'd like to audition for the show. Jim recalled what happened. "Lawrence phoned and said, 'Can you be here today?' You can't imagine what a shock it was to hear his familiar voice asking me to come sing for him. I believed I had something unique to offer because I'm a self-contained act and I do country music, so I knew I wouldn't be duplicating any of the other acts on the show."

Jim sang for Mr. Welk at his home then auditioned for the staff and was hired as a regular in 1979.

Since the show retired, Jim has done a Broadway show and made numerous personal appearances. Since the middle of 1983 he has been performing his solo act at the Birdcage Square at Knott's Berry Farm in Buena Park, California. He recently released a new solo country album entitled "Earthtones." Fans everywhere can expect to see and hear a lot more of Jim Turner.

Recipe for Remembrance

"Music has always been a part of me. I've always felt very spiritual about God-given talents. I've always known if the Lord desired, I would spend my life developing those talents. It was what I yearned to do and I tried to listen to His guidance, so here I am."

Recipes

When Cinda interviewed Jim, he was eating a "brought home" sandwich and salad. He claims he never cooks because he's too busy, but came up with recipes for two very healthy delicious meals to contribute to our cause. Jim's Tennessee Tacos are very simple. He arranges all of the ingredients buffet style so friends can make their own. He says they're messy to eat but terribly tasty. Jim's Breakfast Drink is a health food dream, guaranteed to supply energy and nutrition.

The Sauerkraut Salad and Coconut Kisses are from Jim's mother, Georgia Turner, who lives in Knoxville, Tennessee. She grew up in Berne, Indiana, which is a Swiss colony, and married a true southern gentleman, so combines southern with German and Swiss cooking.

SAUERKRAUT SALAD

Salad
1 cup drained sauerkraut
1 cup celery, finely chopped
¼ cup green pepper, diced
1 (4 ounce) jar pimentos
¼ cup onion, finely chopped
Dressing
1 cup sugar
⅓ cup cider vinegar

Combine sugar and vinegar and boil for 15 minutes. Cool. Combine all salad ingredients then pour cooled dressing over the sauerkraut mixture and chill for 3 to 4 hours before serving. Serves 4.

COCONUT KISSES

1 cup sugar
4 egg whites
1 cup coconut
1 cup nuts (your choice)
3 cups corn flakes

Separate eggs and beat whites until stiff. Gradually add sugar, coconut, nuts and corn flakes. Stir until mixed well then drop from teaspoon onto slightly greased baking sheet. Bake at 325 degrees for 20 minutes. Cool before removing from baking sheet.

JIM'S TENNESSEE TACOS

onions
tomatoes
green peppers
green olives
fresh spinach
ground sirloin
medium sharp cheddar cheese, grated
corn tortillas

Finely chop the desired quantity of the following ingredients: onions, tomatoes, green peppers, green olives, and fresh spinach. Grate medium sharp cheddar cheese and brown ground sirloin. Sizzle each corn tortilla in hot oil long enough to heat but do not make crispy. Drain on a paper towel to absorb excess oil. Fill with whatever ingredients please your taste buds.

JIM'S BREAKFAST DRINK

1 banana
16 ounces orange juice
2 Tbsp. debittered, flaked, brewer's yeast
2 Tbsp. 100% soybean protein powder
2 Tbsp. raw wheat germ
(These ingredients are available in health food stores.)

Blend in blender to desired consistency and drink.

Rose Weiss

Talented Rose Weiss was costume designer for the Lawrence Welk
Show for twenty-five years. Her behind-the-scenes artistry was
appreciated by fans everywhere from the moment she started designing
costumes and outfitting the entire cast for nationwide television. She was re-

sponsible for making Lawrence Welk the "Dapper Dan" of big band conductors and her original creations lent an air of authenticity and beauty to each production.

Rose attended Wayne University for Theater Arts in Detroit, Michigan and sang and performed in little theater in Detroit. After moving to the west coast, she took more theater art classes at Santa Monica City College and performed in The Children's Theater there for three years. She worked for ABC television for eighteen years on various shows, while doing the Lawrence Welk Show. She costumed ten Oscar telecasts and traveled with Bob Hope's overseas Christmas shows from 1968 to 1972 as a costumer. She has been with Teleklew Productions since 1977.

Rose's husband of 43 years, David Weiss, buys and sells Army surplus. They have two sons. Cory is a lawyer and Brian owns restaurants and is a real estate developer.

Recipe

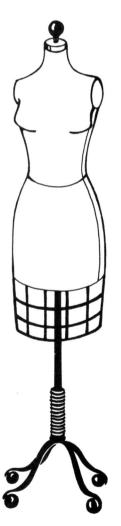

Rose gave us a recipe that originally belonged to her mother. She suggests you serve Noodle Kugel in place of rice or potatoes.

NOODLE KUGEL

1 (12 ounce) package medium width
   noodles
4 eggs (warmed to room temperature)
6 McIntosh or Green Pippin apples
2 (6 ounce) cans undiluted orange juice
   concentrate
½ cup sugar
½ cup (1 cube) butter
½ tsp. cinnamon
¼ cup white raisins
1 tsp. vanilla extract

Cook noodles according to package directions. Drain. Peel and thinly slice the apples. Beat eggs then add all remaining ingredients except the butter. Fold in noodles. Melt the butter in a 9" x 13"x 2" baking dish and pour in batter. Bake at 350 degrees for 1 hour, until top is brown and crisp.

Lawrence and Rose, bubbly as ever!

Laura and Johnny

Johnny Zell

Johnny Zell has been playing the trumpet for most of his life. He first auditioned for the Lawrence Welk Show when he was fifteen years old. Lawrence thought he was too young, but told Johnny to come around and see him again when he was a bit older and had more experience.

143

"So after I graduated from high school I joined the Army and played in the Army Band for three years," Johnny explained.

"During that time I was asked to do a commercial for Army recruiting. As part of the promotion I was supposed to do an interview for the Welk Show and play my trumpet with the band." After Johnny performed with the group, Lawrence held a job open for him for thirteen months until he finished his time in the service.

John was introduced to his beautiful and talented wife Laura by Tom Netherton. Their first date was to a taping of the show. They dated for 4½ years before getting married, but started performing together before they said "I do." Laura is also his accompanist and has done some of their arrangements. Their first child, Colette, was born in March of 1983.

Presently, the Zells are involved in a Gospel ministry, doing Christian concerts around the country, as well as making albums. To the delight of his many fans, John intends to pursue both his Christian and secular music career.

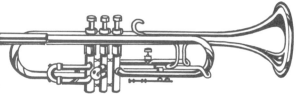

Recipe for Remembrance

"A lot of humorous things happened when I was on the show. One that may haunt me forever is the way Lawrence pronounced my name. He'd always say, 'And here is our young trumpet player, Johnny Sells,' or Cells, instead of Johnny Zell. So to this day, my fan mail is still often addressed to Johnny Sells."

Encino, California. Not only is it mouth-wateringly delicious but simple, fast, and easy to prepare, and always receives rave reviews.

Recipes

Johnny answered a quick and unequivocal NO! when asked if he cooks, but admitted that he sometimes does dishes or putters around in the kitchen, so Laura gets credit for submitting these delicous recipes. She first prepared Mousaka, a Greek casserole, for neighbors who are vegetarians. "I didn't want to do the traditional pasta, so came up with the Mousaka."

The cheesecake is a family recipe, given to her by her mother, Elnora Semeniuk, of

Johnny and the Maestro

MOUSAKA

1 brown onion
1 Tbsp. margarine or salad oil
2 fresh, peeled, diced tomatoes
½ cup sliced mushrooms
1 eggplant
8 ounces sliced, Swiss cheese
Parmesan cheese
Salt and pepper
Pinch of basil or oregano

Preheat oven to 350 degrees. Brown the onion in margarine or salad oil. Add tomatoes, mushrooms, and salt and pepper to taste. Sauté for one minute. Peel and cut eggplant into slices that are ½ inch thick. Brush with salad oil and broil each side until golden brown. Layer into a 9" x 13" x 2" casserole as follows.

First layer: Place eggplant slices in casserole and sprinkle with salt and pepper and a pinch of basil or oregano.

Second layer: Cover the eggplant with the onion mixture.

Third layer: Top with Swiss cheese slices and sprinkle with Parmesan.

Repeat the procedure until all ingredients

are used. Sprinkle Parmesan cheese on the top and bake ½ hour at 350 degrees. Serves 4–6.

Laura suggests serving this nutritious dish with your favorite salad, perhaps a gelatin mold, and fruit or Italian ice for dessert.

VEGETABLE QUICHE

2 cups chopped broccoli or cauliflower
½ cup chopped onion
½ cup chopped green pepper
1 cup shredded cheddar cheese
1½ cups milk
3 eggs
¾ cup biscuit mix
1 tsp. salt
¼ tsp. black pepper

Preheat oven to 400 degrees. Cook broccoli for 5 minutes. Drain and add onion, green pepper, cheese, salt and pepper, and mix. Pack loosely into a greased, 10 inch pie plate. Beat together the milk, eggs, biscuit mix, and salt and pepper and pour over the vegetable crust. Bake 40 to 45 minutes, until golden brown and a knife inserted in the center comes out clean. Let stand 10 minutes before serving. Serves 4–6.

Laura and Colette

ELNORA'S CHEESECAKE

8 ounce carton of non-dairy whipped topping
4 ounces cream cheese
3 Tbsp. sour cream
4 Tbsp. sugar
½ tsp. salt
1 tsp. vanilla

Blend cheese, sour cream, sugar, salt, and vanilla until smooth. Fold in whipped topping. Pour into a cool graham cracker crust and refrigerate. Top with cherries or your favorite berry.

To prepare the crust, blend 1 cup graham cracker crumbs, 4 Tbsp. softened butter, and 2 Tbsp. sugar. Pat firmly into a 9" pie plate. Broil for 2 minutes.

SPANISH SALSA

½ cup broccoli
½ cup cauliflower (optional)
1 rib celery
3 brown onions
1 clove garlic
1 bunch cilandro leaves
⅔ tsp. Jalapeno peppers, fresh or canned
½ tsp. sugar
5 fresh tomatoes
1 8-ounce can tomato sauce
salt and pepper

Finely chop all ingredients. (We found that water chopping in a blender worked well and was a time saver.) Pour into a large bowl. Add tomato sauce, sugar, and salt to taste. Mix well. This salsa tastes best when served at room temperature. Great with tortilla chips, corn chips, or crackers.

Colette

Johnny and Colette

Norma Zimmer

Listening to the brilliant voice of Champagne Lady Norma Zimmer was always a special treat for fans of the Lawrence Welk Show. Norma became a member of the Musical Family on the 1960 New Year's Eve show. She explained how she got this key position. "For about four or five years before I appeared on the show I was singing the La-La-La's and Ba-Ba-Ba's on the background of Mr. Welk's albums, so I knew him. George Cates, who was his music supervisor in those days, kept telling Lawrence about me and he would always say, 'Yes, yes, but I've heard a lot of pretty voices.' Then we did a Thanksgiving album where I sang a tiny four-bar solo and finally, Lawrence took note and invited me to appear on the television show. All I was supposed to sing was that four-bar solo. The Lord worked things out for me that day because Joe Feeney got laryngitis, so that opened a spot for me to sing a whole song."

Norma sang "Smoke Gets In Your Eyes," for her premiere performance. The audience reaction was so positive, Mr. Welk kept inviting her back, strictly as a week-to-week employee, then finally invited her to join the Musical Family on a permanent basis at the beginning of 1960.

Life hasn't always been so glamorous for Norma. She was born in Idaho on a dairy farm in a tiny log cabin. When she was about two years old, her father moved the family to Tacoma, Washington, where he was an engraver. They later located in Seattle. "We were really poor," Norma noted, "because my father was a violin teacher during the depression years. Of course, nobody had money for music lessons, so he would give lessons in exchange for medical treatment for the family. He would go to a vegetable stand and bring home the outside leaves of the produce. We barely existed and went hungry a lot of times."

Norma and her husband, Randy, were married in 1945. A devoted wife and mother, she loves to talk about her husband and family. "Randy and I had such a romantic meeting. I went skiing with a girlfriend in Washington State. We had to take the bus and as I stepped off the bus, here was this beautiful hunk of man standing outside the door. My girlfriend knew him and introduced us. I couldn't say a word because my heart was doing flip-flops."

"I was a rank beginner skier and Randy was racing for the northwest championship at that time. My girlfriend and I were staying at a cabin that her friends owned and we couldn't get the fireplace going. Smoke bellowed into the cabin and some of the fellows from the ski club Randy belonged to invited us to spend the night at the girl's dorm. We did, and in the morning when I went down to breakfast in the cafeteria Randy was there and offered to teach me to ski. I don't understand how he could even have noticed me a second time. I didn't have ski clothes; we couldn't afford them, so I was wearing my girlfriend's mother's outfit. She weighed maybe twenty to twenty-five pounds more than I and was six inches taller. You can imagine how I looked!"

Norma is also a proud mother and grandmother. The Zimmers have two wonderful sons. Mark, who is still a bachelor, is a computer program analyst. Their oldest son, Ron, and his wife, Candy, who is a nurse, have three children. In Norma's words, "They have two charming, beautiful, lovely, gorgeous daughters, Kristin and Amanda," and presented Norma and Randy with their first grandson, Andrew Jason, in March of 1984.

As for the future, Norma intends to "keep doing concerts as long as the Lord will let me sing." She performs all around the country and does guest appearances on Christian television programs. She is studying voice again because, "As we get older our voices change and there's always room for improvement." Norma is an excellent artist with some of her paintings on tour with celebrity art exhibits. She feels it's the perfect artistic outlet when she is not singing.

Norma and Randy make their home in La Habra, California.

Recipe for Remembrance

We asked Norma to reflect on her success and tell us one secret that she has found especially helpful when dealing with the constant demands on a celebrity. "When I was a young girl I was told that I looked pretty when I smiled. That started me smiling for the rest of my life. A smile does for a homely face what flowers do for a humble home. I like smiling people, and I want to be one, too."

Like all of the other performers, Norma has many warm and humorous memories about the Musical Family. "Lawrence is a great tease and I'm very serious about my work. I have always been a perfectionist and if it isn't right I just don't want to be there. One time, after I had finished singing a song, he came over to me with this very sad, serious expression on his face and said, 'Norma, I don't think we can use that number on the show.' Of course, I was heartbroken. Then he got that twinkle in his eye and started laughing and stamping his foot. He was always teasing."

Recipes

Norma says she and Randy try to stay as close as possible to what God intended us to eat. "We eat very simply. Since the kids have gone, I don't ever make anything sweet and I keep very few fattening things in the house. We hike five miles every morning. We get up at daybreak and walk so that we can start the day's activities at the

Norma and Randy

usual hour. And, I do a few stretching exercises."

Norma loves to entertain, so she shared two of her favorite "company" recipes. The Beef Stroganoff is her mother's recipe. She says it's fabulous and so simple, and suggests that you use fillet because it is so tender. She serves her stroganoff over wild rice, to which she's added some chopped green onion tips and cashews. French style green beans seasoned with bacon bits, sautéed celery and onion, and a bit of butter make a perfect side dish. For the finishing touch, Norma serves cheese bread and ends the meal with a simple dessert like ice cream sundaes.

Chicken Salad is the dish that inspired Cinda Redman to compile this cookbook when Norma served it at a luncheon.

Avid skiers, Randy and Norma

BEEF STROGANOFF

8 beef fillets, cut into small pieces
3 (10¾ ounce) cans cream of mushroom
soup
1 cup fresh, sliced mushrooms OR
1 jar drained, button mushrooms
2 pints sour cream

Sauté the beef in butter and salt until ten-der. Do not overcook. Add the soup and mushrooms and mix well. Set aside. Just before serving add the sour cream. Heat well but do not boil or the cream will curdle. Serves 6–8.

CHICKEN SALAD

5 cups cooked chicken breasts, boned and
diced
2 cups pineapple chunks, drained
¾ cup toasted almonds or cashews
2 cups seedless grapes
2 cups celery, diced
1 cup mayonnaise
1 cup sour cream
1 tsp. curry powder
1 tsp. salt

Combine the chicken, pineapple, nuts, grapes, and celery in a large salad bowl. Mix together the mayonnaise, sour cream, and seasonings. Stir into the salad mixture and chill well. Serve over leaf lettuce. Serves 4–6.

Norma holding new grandson Andrew Jason, surrounded by (clockwise) Amanda, Randy, Ron, Mark, Kristin and Candy

Index of Recipes

153

D.C. al Fine